ST. WERBURGH'S AND ALL SAINTS'.

IN COLSTON'S DAYS

A STORY OF OLD BRISTOL

BY

EMMA MARSHALL
AUTHOR OF "LIFE'S AFTERMATH"

SEVENTH THOUSAND

LONDON
SEELEY AND CO. LIMITED
38 Great Russell Street
1907

TO THE

DEAR AND HONOURED MEMORY

OF

JOHN ADDINGTON SYMONDS, M.D.,

WHO IN HIS DAY AND GENERATION

ADDED SO GREATLY TO THE PROSPERITY OF CLIFTON,

BY ATTRACTING THITHER MANY, IN WHOSE HEARTS HE STILL LIVES

BY HIS RARE MEDICAL SKILL,

HIS HIGH CULTURE AND INTELLECTUAL GIFTS,

AND HIS EVER-READY HOSPITALITY,

WHICH MADE CLIFTON HILL HOUSE, WITH ITS TREASURES OF

ART AND LITERATURE,

THE CENTRE OF ALL THAT WAS BRIGHT, BEAUTIFUL, AND GOOD

I DEDICATE THIS STORY OF

OLD BRISTOL,

AS A TOKEN OF UNCHANGING AFFECTION.

PREFACE.

"THE days of the years" of the great Bristol philanthropist cover a wide area, and **it is** therefore impossible to do more than bring into the story of his times the salient points of his long life.

I have ventured to throw round the early youth of Edward Colston the halo of romance —not, indeed, following in the track of the many stories which are told of his love, and the causes of its rejection by the woman of his choice. For, as not one of these stories is confessedly reliable, I have taken leave to invent one, on the ground of probability, but with no pretence of certainty. I think, however, we may reasonably suppose that the life of this great man was coloured by the love of some woman, who may have quickened in him the universal benevolence which made the widow and the orphan his especial care. Thus I have assumed, that this unrequited love of his, was centred on a noble, gracious woman, who, though for her own reasons refusing to be his wife, yet influenced him for good;—rather than on a selfish and frivolous one, who, as one of the popular stories to which I have referred sets forth, refused to be his wife on the plea of his lavish generosity to a poor suppliant for charity in the streets of Bristol.

Edward Colston's affection for his mother, and devotion to the memory of both parents, must naturally take a prominent place in any story of his early life; and we may imagine that a mother so dearly loved must have been—as all true mothers should strive to be—the sympathetic friend and the counsellor of her first-born son.

The characters I have introduced are, I need hardly say, for the most part wholly imaginary. At the same time, I have borrowed names from the old records of Bristol; and when I have dealt with facts and historical events in which the city of the west had its part, I have carefully adhered to verified dates, and done my best to keep the action of the story within the limits of the time when such events really took place.

All that is known with any certainty of the man, of whom Bristol is justly proud, is to be found in Mr. Thomas Garrard's life, ably edited by Mr. Tovey.

I have to acknowledge my obligations to that work, and also to the three beautiful volumes entitled " Bristol : Past and Present," which ought to be in the library of every one who wishes to realise the history of this ancient city.

I must also express my thanks to Miss Emily Holt for her valuable information as to the costumes of the period—a subject which, with its Christian names, she has studied so carefully, that she is an undoubted and reliable authority upon it, and many other like questions of interest, connected with the past of her country.

The illustrations—sketches from some of the old buildings which remain in Bristol—may add to the interest of the tale. These old buildings, alas! are becoming less and less in number, as streets are widened and new thoroughfares opened out, to meet the requirements of modern life.

But no changes can blot out the memory of the man who bravely rose as the champion of education in a time when it was thought a "grave error in judgment" to teach the son and daughter of the mechanic and tradesman to read and write. His work lives: it reaches far back into the past, and it stretches out to the future. Many brave and useful men have traced the beginning of their career to Colston's School; and may we not hope that in the time to come these shall be followed by others, who shall bear witness to the truth of the words of the wise man?—for "the good name" of the Bristol philanthropist is better than his "great riches."

10, WORCESTER TERRACE, CLIFTON,
All Saints' Day, 1883.

CONTENTS.

BOOK I.

	PAGE
IN THE CRADLE	3
A CHURCH WITH A CHIMNEY	19
THE GREAT HOUSE ON THE BRIDGE	38

BOOK II.

SUMMER DAYS	67
A HUNTED HARE	93
ON THE RIVER	109
ROYAL ROBES	126

BOOK III.

A WOMAN'S MESSAGE	199

BOOK IV.

THE END OF THE JOURNEY	235
THE GREAT HOUSE	282
FOR WHIG OR TORY?	305
A LAUREL CROWN	315
THE RETURN	328

BOOK I.

IN THE CRADLE.

There is a history in all men's lives,
Figuring the nature of the times deceased,
The which observed, a man may prophesy
With a near aim, of the main chance of things,
As yet not come to life, which in their seeds
And weak beginnings lie intreasured.

Shakespeare.

BOOK I.

DECEMBER, 1636.

IN THE CRADLE.

The sun was setting in a sky, which was painted with every shade of amethyst and gold, ethereal green, and tenderest sapphire, melting into opal tints of indescribable loveliness.

A few detached clouds floated over the old city of Bristol, sent as messengers from the sunset; their snowy breasts were tinged with bright crimson, and reflected a ruddy glow upon the dull waters of the Avon, flowing swiftly out under the arches of the bridge, seaward; while the cross on the chapel dedicated to the Virgin, midway on the crowded thoroughfare, shone like a ruby set in gold. In the year of grace 1636, Bristol Bridge was a narrow street, with houses built on either side, and the chapel, raised over a vaulted arch under which carriages could pass, stood in the centre. Of all the busy streets in Old Bristol, the bridge was perhaps the busiest. Many of the rich merchants lived here, above their stores and low shops, where much weighty business was transacted, of which the selling of wares was the least important. The Bristol merchants were, even at this date, deep in the gains and losses of foreign ventures and trading with Spain and Portugal, while representatives of most of the leading houses were to be found in Madrid, Oporto, and in the islands which in the last century had tempted many a brave adventurer over the great Atlantic to seek his fortune in the El Dorado of the West.

The houses on the bridge had the advantage over the houses in the narrow streets, for the backs commanded a fine prospect either way along the river, while the houses in the streets, often spacious and highly decorated within, could from the projecting lattice bays, but dimly discern a strip of sky between the roofs, and but glimpses of what was passing at the opening of the narrow street at either end.

Although scarcely half-past three of the clock it was nearly dark in St. Mary le Port Street. The glories of the winter sunset could not penetrate the dim spacious room in the house of Master Thomas Standfast, where, in the wide lattice bay window, his little daughter

Damaris had been keeping watch for a long time. Damaris pressed her face close to the window, and peered out steadily in one direction, now and then changing her position from the left foot to the right, and playing a tune upon the diamond panes with her small fingers.

OLD BRISTOL BRIDGE.

The room behind her was dark and gloomy. The oak panels were not relieved by any colour, and a tall bureau, with brass fittings, alone caught the flickering of the wood fire now burning low on the wide hearth. The oak boards were polished and slippery; they were covered here and there by strips or squares of carpet, and the straight-backed chairs stood, like sentinels, against the walls. A piece of heavy and moth-eaten tapestry hung over a door at the further end of the room, and by it, away from the fire, sat a young woman who was dressed in a coarse brown stuff gown, with a muslin kerchief crossed on her breast, and her hands busily employed with the distaff, while her foot occasionally touched the wooden cradle where a baby was asleep.

The window where Damaris stood was raised a step from the room, and from her superior elevation the child looked down, as well as back, at the figure by the tapestry, and said, in a quick petulant voice,

"I am sick of waiting; mother will never come from the christening feast. Thou art like a mole or a bat, Cicely, working in the dark. Leave thy stupid distaff, and come here and look out. There is a tiny cloud just over the top of the cross beyond Master Aldworth's house. It is rosy red; come and see it."

"I fear to wake thy sister; she has been over fretful, and slept not a wink last night. Talk not so loud, Damaris."

"Come near then, and I will whisper." And as the girl's figure moved softly across the room and emerged from the shadows, Damaris continued, "That's a good Cicely; now tell me why my mother should don her very best flowered taffety and velvet kirtle, and make such an ado as to her ornaments, and strut up and down to be admired forsooth, and leave me dull at home? I should have liked a chrisom feast, and to have beheld all the fine things at Master Colston's. I don't care a whit for the baby. I doubt not he is a little ugly monkey, like the one Will Purdy showed me in the stores the other day. Moreover, we have got a baby here. I hate a fuss—about babies!"

"Damaris, thy idle words make a long account; thy tongue wants a bridle."

"Nay, Cicely, thou canst not tell how I crave for my own mother. Dost think *she* would have pranked herself out in finery, and stepped out to the christening, nor taken me with her? My blessed mother, who is safe with the holy angels! I need her sore."

"Dear child, I know thou dost often need her; but oh! Damaris, methinks she is taken from the evil to come. There are no times of peace before us, but rather dread times. The enemies of the Lord are gathering for the battle, and we know not where it will end. For myself, I would not go anear a chrisom feast, nor taste one of the viands, for it seemeth to me a fearful mockery to mark the child's brow with the sign of the cross which he will never take up, nursed in the lap of luxury and godlessness."

Cicely's face, which had been so quiet and unmoved a minute before, was now aglow with a strange light.

"Thou should'st hear Mistress Dorothy on this matter."

"That will I not. I love her not. With her groans about sin, and her long face and whines. I love her not. And when she comes here preaching at mother, I would as lieve tell her to let the minister speak of such things, and mind her own affairs. Father cannot abide her; he said so."

Cicely only sighed, and her sweet face resumed its usually placid expression.

"Thy father loveth peace," sighed Cicely; "but hark, it is the child stirring."

Cicely stepped down from the raised daïs by the window, and taking the baby in her arms caressed it lovingly.

"Now then, sweetheart, do not fret; come

and see thy sister. Sure, Damaris, a child more like an angel never lived in this sin-struck world. Alas! that she is a child of wrath, and doomed to punishment, if God's grace fall not on her."

This stern doctrine did not seem to fall naturally from those sweet serene lips.

"Here," said Damaris, "let me dandle her, it will pass the time till they return."

She took the child rather roughly from Cicely's arms, and tried to amuse her by shaking the beads of her necklace, and swaying her backwards and forwards.

The baby, little Margery, lay quite quiet, with her blue eyes raised to the light, still seen through the roofs of the houses. The babies of those days were swathed in garments which gave but little room for stretching their limbs. They wore tightly-fitting caps, from under which the soft rings of golden hair made a fringe round little Margery's fair forehead.

Damaris, at scarcely ten years old, was dressed as a woman, in stuff petticoat and over garment of flowered camlet, her gay kerchief girt in at the waist by a broad belt. She wore on her dark hair something between a snood and a cap, and had a falling fringe of gilt beads, enemies of the Lord are gathering for the battle, and we know not where it will end. For myself, I would not go anear a chrisom feast, nor taste one of the viands, for it seemeth to me a fearful mockery to mark the child's brow with the sign of the cross which he will never take up, nursed in the lap of luxury and godlessness."

Cicely's face, which had been so quiet and unmoved a minute before, was now aglow with a strange light.

"Thou should'st hear Mistress Dorothy on this matter."

"That will I not. I love her not. With her groans about sin, and her long face and whines. I love her not. And when she comes here preaching at mother, I would as lieve tell her to let the minister speak of such things, and mind her own affairs. Father cannot abide her; he said so."

Cicely only sighed, and her sweet face resumed its usually placid expression.

"Thy father loveth peace," sighed Cicely; "but hark, it is the child stirring."

Cicely stepped down from the raised daïs by the window, and taking the baby in her arms caressed it lovingly.

"Now then, sweetheart, do not fret; come

and see thy sister. Sure, Damaris, a child more like an angel never lived in this sin-struck world. Alas! that she is a child of wrath, and doomed to punishment, if God's grace fall not on her."

This stern doctrine did not seem to fall naturally from those sweet serene lips.

"Here," said Damaris, "let me dandle her, it will pass the time till they return."

She took the child rather roughly from Cicely's arms, and tried to amuse her by shaking the beads of her necklace, and swaying her backwards and forwards.

The baby, little Margery, lay quite quiet, with her blue eyes raised to the light, still seen through the roofs of the houses. The babies of those days were swathed in garments which gave but little room for stretching their limbs. They wore tightly-fitting caps, from under which the soft rings of golden hair made a fringe round little Margery's fair forehead.

Damaris, at scarcely ten years old, was dressed as a woman, in stuff petticoat and over garment of flowered camlet, her gay kerchief girt in at the waist by a broad belt. She wore on her dark hair something between a snood and a cap, and had a falling fringe of gilt beads, which had belonged to her mother, hanging from it at the back.

"She is fairer to look on than the baby in Small Street, I'll warrant, though I do account her a plague at times. I'll allow she is comely enough. There, Cicely, art satisfied now? It is getting so dark I can scarce see one from another below. Ha! there is Will Purdy out gaping, and there's the flicker of a torch. They are coming now. Take thy babe, Cicely, and let me go to meet mother."

"Madam Standfast, at your service," Damaris said, with a low curtsey, as she threw open the heavy door, and a lady, hooded and covered with a long cloak, entered with a waiting-maid, who was Mistress Standfast's especial property, as she had brought her to her new home as her only dower when she consented to be the second wife of Thomas Standfast.

"Well, I've had enow," she said, " of this christening, but it was mighty grand. Take my cloak and hood, Hannah, and bring in a cup of water with a dash of canary in it. I am ready to drop."

"Tell us about it, mother," Damaris said, taking a tabouret and sitting down at her mother's feet. "Tell us all about it. I've had a dull day and I'd have liked to be there. This Mistress Colston said—"

"Tush, prythee, silly child, thou art old enow for thy ten years, and dost not need bringing forward. One thing I can tell thee, that Colonel Taylor swore there was no dress to beat mine. He asked where I got this gold brocade, and said he never saw such a fitting robe for one who walked like a swan. Ha, ha! how men will flatter," and Mistress Standfast arched her pretty neck, and patted the costly lace which filled in the somewhat low bodice.

Damaris shrugged her shoulders, and said, "We have seen your gown, and heard of its grandeur ere now; tell us of the company, mother."

"The company—oh, they were not amiss, and the room where the banquet was spread is a grand one. Master Colston must be getting money by ship-loads. A fine marriage for Counsellor Batten's daughter. The baby had a grand christening robe, and he screeched thrice, they said, at Temple Church, when he felt the water. He seems a weakly child, and his mother said she would have fain had him plunged in, and not sprinkled only. They are mighty stiff church folk, and it's better so, than to be like those ill-conditioned people, of the Kelly set, who think all the town will go to perdition but their precious selves. Ah! Cicely looks as if she would place me with the goats. How has the baby Margery prospered? Is she less restive?"

"She is as good as gold, madam," was Cicely's demure answer.

The baby's lady mother touched the soft cheek with her fingers, and said,

"I am pleased to see she hath little golden ringlets. We will marry her to the babe in Small Street, eh, Thomas?"

"A fine match for her, doubtless," said the good tradesman and merchant, Thomas Standfast. "There's magic in the way the Colstons prosper—"

"Father," broke in Damaris, "I want to hear about the christening feast, and all the folks did and said and wore, and mother only tells me about herself, and that is dull."

"Hush thy pert tongue, Damaris, lest I send thee to bed with a crust and a flagon of water," said Thomas Standfast.

But Madam Standfast only laughed, and tossed her pretty head.

"Nay, I do not fret about the girl's tongue; I

have something else to do. Did'st hear Colonel Taylor's pretty speech to me? 'Easy to see,' quoth he, 'that you have gentle blood in your veins, fair lady.' And quoth I, 'You are quick-sighted, sir, for in good sooth I come of the blood of the FitzHardinges, though the wife of a Bristol merchant, by your leave.' 'Ah,' quoth my fine gentleman, 'the Bristol merchants are fast becoming the princes of the earth.' And he added, 'Some of the said princes are like to come down a bit: for there is more to be heard of ship money yet.'"

"Tut-tut! What do womenfolk know of these matters? Tell us about the gauds, and the comfits, and the brave gowns, and leave prating to such goodwives as Dolly Kelly."

Thomas Standfast had put his arm round Damaris and drew her to his side.

"The babe was brought in at the banquet," he said, "and his mother handed him round to each guest, who kissed him on the cheek, and offered a gift. Some were mighty fine, and such rare apostle's spoons, chased and finely wrought, I never saw. They must have cost a fortune. The shining of the plate on the board was grand to see, and there was a preserve of some sweet juicy fruit, which I would fain have got into my pocket for thee. I brought this, however; and the kind young mistress bid me present it with her dutiful compliments to my little daughter, and she prayed me to send thee and the baby Margery to kiss her boy before many days pass." Thomas Standfast drew from one of the large pockets of his short coat a large slice of cake—all sugar and spice —and as dark and rich as any cake that was ever made.

"Kind father!" Damaris exclaimed, throwing her arms round her father's neck. "Always kind."

"Thy Uncle Dick was a guest, and spoke well at the drinking of healths. He has the gift of the tongue, which thy father has not. They were mostly elderly folks present—grandparents and grand-aunts of the babe. The youngest present was the mother—a most fair young mother, and so proud of her boy."

Thomas Standfast sighed; he was thinking of past days, when Damaris lay in her mother's arms, and she sang soft and low, to hush her to sleep in the twilight.

Now as the baby Margery began to make little pitiful noises, for she was cutting her first teeth, the fine lady mother, in whose veins coursed noble blood, exclaimed, "Take her away, Cicely. I cannot bear to hear her whine. I mislike her when she puckers up her face."

Madam Standfast thought it her bounden duty to show her high lineage by calmly ignoring her maternal duties. A spoiled beauty, left an orphan and friendless, she had touched the heart of the worthy Thomas Standfast, who had been a faithful widower for six years, when he married, for the second time, Mistress Margaret FitzHardinge, whose father had been a scion of the younger branch of the Berkleys, and had died early, leaving a widow and daughter in very straitened circumstances.

Thomas Standfast assisted the mother to eke out her scanty income by investing her slender capital in his flourishing business, and at her death Mistress Margaret and her waiting-maid, Hannah, were received into his house, and found a comfortable home—the one as wife, the other as servant.

Madam Standfast was poor in all things but beauty and pride. Of these she had a goodly supply. She was vain and selfish, but so equable was her temper, and so quiet her self-assertion that she managed to pass for a sweet-tempered woman. She had everything her own way, was contradicted by no one, and flattered by the admiration of Thomas Standfast's household. The only openly professed unbeliever in Madam Standfast's perfections was her step-daughter, Damaris. But when her eyes flashed and her spirit rose, or her tongue ran beyond the ordinary limit, from some great provocation, it was she who always bore the brunt of her father's indignation, and her step-mother got off scot free. Not that anything Damaris could say or do affected Madam Standfast. She cared far too little about her, or any one but herself, to be deeply moved by anything Damaris might say. But if she could be provoked into betraying irritation it was on the subject of age and beauty.

Her husband's praise of Madam Colston annoyed her, and when after a pause he repeated:

"Yes, Mistress Batten is fair enow and young withal. May she be spared to be a blessing to her boy and his father for many long years!"

"Fair and young! Well-a-day! I am as young as Madam Colston; and as to fair, I fancy no one calls me a fright." Then she laughed her little laugh, which, heard for the first time, might sound silvery, but when heard often, had a ring in it, which was monotonous, and suggestive of no very deep spring of happiness.

"Sarah Batten may be older than she looks."

"And why call her Sarah Batten? It sounds strangely."

"It is long usage, methinks," said her husband. "I say she may be older than she looks; but her face to-day, as she bore that infant round amongst her kinsfolk and friends, was as pure and child-like as our little Margery's."

"I do not affect baby faces on old shoulders. Now I must away and let Hannah smoothe my train and fold it in the chest." She stood up as she said so, and turned her graceful head from side to side, and passed out of the room behind the tapestry with the easy gliding motion of a swan.

"She looks a queen," Thomas Standfast said. "Aye, Damaris, too much of a queen for a Bristol merchant. Supper will be served ere long, methinks. The lads below have had a long fast, and I must away and look into matters before supper."

"Father," Damaris said, "Will Purdy takes it ill that mother will not eat with the apprentices oftener than she can help. Prythee let me come down with thee. It has been a long, long day."

"So do then, dear child, and mind thee that my Lady Rogers bids thee to the Bridge House to-morrow."

Damaris jumped for joy.

"I never heard it. I am right glad."

"Thy mother forgot to tell thee, perhaps. Dame Rogers is willing to teach thee some new tapestry stitch and embroidery."

"I hate the needle," Damaris said, "though I love to go to these grand houses and look out on the river. It is mighty dull here since Cicely has taken to Mistress Kelly's ways."

"And my Lady Rogers is bitten with the same disease; for, child, it is for us to follow humbly in the ways of our fathers, delivered from Popery, for which thank God; but to keep in good old paths by the ancient discipline of the Church. And now come, as it pleases you, to my lower chamber. I can give thee some strange pictures I found in an old chest of yams, brought in from Saint Kit's by the good skipper, Jordan by name."

A CHURCH WITH A CHIMNEY.

WHILE Damaris goes with her father to the lower floor of the house, and, seated on a high stool at a desk in the inner shop or office, delighted with the quaint treasures which Thomas Standfast always preserved for his little daughter, Cicely Knight, the nurse and caretaker of little Margery, was passing down the wide staircase, wrapt in a long dark mantle, and her head covered with a hood. At the foot of the stairs the head apprentice of Thomas Standfast's business, Will Purdy, was waiting for her.

"Hast thou asked leave, Will?" Cecily said.

"No, there is no need. I shall be back ere supper is served."

"I would as lief the good master knew of thy absence, Will."

"Doth the lady mistress know of thine?" retorted Will.

"Aye, verily. I craved two hours' freedom

from my duties, alleging I had slept ill with the care of the babe yesternight."

"Then thy leave will halve itself right easily, and I'll take the lesser portion and thou shalt take the lion's share, fair Cicely—my Cicely, eh?" he continued, trying to take her hand. But Cicely withdrew it quickly.

"Nay, then, Will. I did not come forth to listen to thy folly. I am on the way to Mistress Dorothy Kelly's, to be fed with the bread of life."

Will laughed.

"Be it so, and drop a few crumbs for me."

"Nay, jest not at so grave a matter. Thou didst promise to come as my guide to Mistress Kelly's, and listen quietly to the godly teaching."

"I will leave thee there and call anon," said Will. "I cannot do more. I am fit to laugh outright when I see these women pulling long faces. Have a care, Cicely!" And Will Purdy put out his hand, and saved his companion from falling over a heap of refuse which was lying in the street. "There, thou hadst need of my hand then! In what a vile condition is this roadway. Small use are your Mayors and Aldermen and Corporation if they cannot make the citizens cleanly and decent in their habits.

They say the Plague is born and bred in these dirty by-ways, and when it visits us again I would fain see the Mayor and Corporation struck with it in their red gowns. It is like to break one's neck and give one a swooning fit to walk abroad in the dark "

Will Purdy, if wrong in his desire for summary vengeance against the Mayor and Corporation of the ancient and loyal city, was right in the estimate he took of Bristol streets. They were at this time as ill-kept, ill-drained, and difficult of passage as it is possible to conceive. The wonder is, not that the Plague seized its prey in Bristol with a fatal grip at longer or shorter intervals, but that the inhabitants of houses like Thomas Standfast's in St. Mary le Port Street were ever well. Certainly it is remarkable that, as a rule, except during the visitations of any great epidemic, there is not any extraordinary death-rate recorded. Indeed, very little is said of health in chronicles of this date. People seemed to thrive, in spite of their surroundings; and when, in about six years from this time, the great rebellion broke out, the men—yes, and the women of Bristol too— showed they were in the full possession of much muscular vigour!

Will Purdy left Cicely at the door of Dorothy Kelly's grocery shop in the High Street just as the clocks were striking six. Dorothy Kelly was in the act of closing her business for the day, by the help of a very meek apprentice, who held his mistress in wholesome awe.

Dorothy Kelly was a remarkable woman of her time. Her presence was commanding, and her tall shapely figure inspired respect. Her features were regular, her brow low and square, and her mouth was set in firm lines. She was the type of the strong, uncompromising Puritan, who with the force of a powerful will, brought weaker ones under complete control. Dorothy Kelly gloried in protesting against what she believed to be unsound doctrine and practices. She set her face as a flint against all expressions of contempt for her favourite creed, and courted rather than avoided persecution "for the truth's sake." Looking back on her figure, as it rises out of the Bristol of those times, we are tempted to wonder why it is, she escaped the persecution unto death which she by no means took any pains to avoid.

Had she not sat serving in her shop as usual

on the Christmas Day preceding that now near at hand, and openly displayed her grocery and spices for sale as on other week-days? Did she not account the observance of the "Christmass" by ringing of bells and services in the church a popish custom to be abhorred by the faithful?

Dorothy paid as little heed to the coarse jest or ironical laughter which her conduct provoked, as to the squealing of Punchinello, in the Bullock's Park. What was it to her, whose salvation was assured, that a crowd of poor sinners should gibe and mock, and disturb the meetings held, as they said, in ' a church with a chimney,' as they called Mrs. Kelly's house in High Street, between the Guilder's Inn and the High Cross?

Cicely was early at Mistress Kelly's, and she stood patiently awaiting an invitation to pass in beyond the shop to a large room which ran lengthwise at the back, and was a convenient and retired place for the meetings of the 'Lord's chosen ones.'

"Well-a-day' exclaimed Mistress Dorothy. "Ah, Cicely, would that the voice of Master Yeamans could be heard this night to call upon the people to turn and repent! It is a shameful thing that in a dwelling of one of our chief merchants, feasting and revelling should follow the popish ceremony of a baptism by water. The judgment of God will fall on Master Colston's children and children's children."

"The babe was baptized in Temple Church, being weakly, soon after its birth in the month of November last," Cicely, who had been standing quietly by the chests and stores piled up just within the threshold of the shop, now ventured to say. "They did but ask their kinsfolk and friends to rejoice that the mother and babe were spared to make glad the hearts of their kindred. Is there harm in this, Mistress Kelly?"

"So you have come to the meeting of the friends of God, and can yet defend the ill-doings of the friends of the world, which two are at enmity? Ah! Cicely, I fear me it is not yet right with your own heart. Pass into the next chamber and see whether the oil is like to hold out in the lamps for two hours. Methinks we shall be exercised to-night for some time, and I would as lieve not be left in darkness.

Cicely did as she was requested, and going through a low passage, entered the room where the meetings were held. It was of fair proportions, for, like many of the houses in old Bristol, Mrs. Kelly's dwelling was far more spacious and roomy than the frontage of the lower floor would lead any one who entered the little shop to suppose.

There was but a dim light in the large chamber of which Cicely softly pushed back the door, and the oil lamps gave a very unpleasant and stifling odour.

The windows, high and difficult of access, were seldom opened, thus the close atmosphere was not surprising.

Cicely trimmed the lamps, pouring in oil from a pipkin which stood by, and then she went to the further end of the room, raised by two steps under the narrow window, and opened the Bible which lay there.

It was just one hundred years ago since the great scholar and martyr of the sixteenth century had given up his life before the Castle of Vilvorde, his only crime the translation of the Word of God into the English tongue. Many storms had convulsed the Church and the kingdom since the days of William Tyndale; but the Bible had survived them all, and was now, as he had desired, an open book wherein he that ran could read, and was a lasting monument of his scholarship and his zeal.

Cicely had taken off her cloak and hood, and stood in her plain gown and snowy kerchief and cap, the very picture of a maiden who had given up all personal adornments and forsaken the vanities of the world. She was, as I have said, a permanent member of Thomas Standfast's household—a distant relation of Damaris's mother. She was received by the worthy merchant as poor relations were received in those days, as a matter of course, in the houses of wealthy citizens and nobles. Cicely Knight's education had been rather above that of the time, and whereas the gay and beautiful wife of Thomas Standfast could scarcely sign her name, and read no book but the book of her own charms and perfections, Cicely, the poor dependent, wrote a fair hand, and read much in the few books which came in her way, especially in the Book on which her slender hand now rested as she turned the pages to the First Epistle of Saint John.

There is no book in the English language which is so calculated to raise the intellectual as well as spiritual tone of those who read it.

The Authorized Version, published in the

reign of the first James, has a beauty of style majestic yet simple, pure yet lofty, which now, when of making books there is no end, strikes us continually with a sense of admiration and wonder. And if so now, how much more when in the seventeenth century, maidens like Cicely Knight had scarcely any other literature within their reach.

The culture of the middle classes was more wholly dependent on the Word of God than we can realize now. And hence it was that the Separatists and Puritans, and a little later the followers of George Fox, acquired a power of speaking in a strain which often rose to the pathos of true poetical expression, and the trenchant style of dramatic power. From this source sprang the immortal allegory from the Bedford prison; and throughout the Pilgrim's Progress there are the unmistakable signs of the writer's frequent contemplation of the vivid pictures of the Revelation by the divine St. John, and of the Lord's teaching on the Mount, and in other places of His earthly ministry.

Cicely's eyes were fixed on the early chapters of St. John's Epistle, and she was repeating aloud in her clear musical voice "God is love.

And he that dwelleth in love dwelleth in God, and God in him." And again, "This is His commandment, that we should love one another."

In this gentle girl's soul there was often stirring a question which she could not satisfactorily answer. This love of God, of which the Apostle spoke—were the brethren and sisters, who judged the world as without their pale, and condemned the Church with its bishops and prelates, following the plain commandment of 'loving one another?' As she thus doubted, and even reproached herself for her doubts, Mistress Dorothy Kelly came in with a young man with a face as fair as a girl's, and of thin spare proportions. He was dressed as a clergyman, and wore a black cassock and cambric neckerchief.

They were followed by Robert Haynes, a writing schoolmaster, and one Richard Moon, a farrier, and Goodman Cole, a butcher. These worthies were the great upholders of the meetings held in Mistress Kelly's house; and when they had taken their seats, a number of less distinguished people were allowed to pass up the narrow passage. Mistress Kelly stood, till every one had entered, and her keen eye was upon each man and woman as they took their places.

Cicely, who had been standing by the desk with the Bible open before her, hastily retreated behind Mistress Kelly and the clergyman, and was half frightened, half glad, to see Will Purdy was one of the last to enter the room.

She did not feel at all sure whether he had come to scoff or to pray, and her fears strengthened when she heard Mistress Kelly in a ringing tone say, " There is a young man down yonder who will find himself t'other side of the door an' he mocks and gibes like a buffoon at a fair."

For Will Purdy had tried to attract Cicely's attention by making the sign of the cross, bowing low in the direction of the table where the Bible lay, and other pantomimic gestures.

Dorothy Kelly waited, never taking her eye off Will Purdy; and as he assumed a demure mien, and seated himself on the end of a bench, she opened the meeting by saying:

"Friends and brethren, and sisters in the Lord, here is a gentleman here to-night who is a stranger and sojourner in this city; he is come to minister at the church of Philip and James next Lord's day. You will give him a hearing, my neighbours, and I warrant he will feed you with something beyond the dry husks of the prelatical teachers—the blind guides of the blind."

This announcement, made with a face lighted up with fiery zeal, seemed a little to confuse the young disciple who stood by Mistress Kelly's side. He might be touched by the spirit of the Puritan, but he was by no means inclined to abuse the Church of which he was a minister. In later times, when under other influences and stirred up to utter the bitter words which seemed to be the badge of Christian earnestness to men and women of Mistress Dorothy's type, he advanced the doctrines which obliged him to give up his "supply" preaching in Redcliff Church, and by the voice of the people of St. Nicholas, secured to himself the cure of souls in that parish.

But this evening, on his first appearance in Bristol, Mr. Hassard felt only a yearning tenderness for the salvation of those before him. When he prayed, the very Spirit of the Lord seemed brought down amongst the listeners. They groaned and agonized in spirit as the petition ascended to God's throne, and they were greatly moved, many of them to tears, by his address.

Will Purdy had listened in spite of himself. And though he was in that assembly but not of it, the preacher had not failed to notice his attentive gaze fixed on his face. The voices of all the meeting were raised at last in a hymn—rugged in metre, and discordant by reason of the different qualities of the voices, which were raised a good deal above the "ordinary pitch."

And now Will Purdy stood as if on guard—looking steadily in the direction of the high windows as if expecting something. Suddenly he sprang forward, seized Cicely by the arm, and before she could resist, or discover what his object was, he had hurried her down the dark narrow passage, while a sound like hail was heard behind them, as the windows were all cracked with stones, and rotten eggs came down on the heads of those at the upper end of the chamber, with dead mice and rats, and such missiles. "I knew they were coming," he said, "that is why I brought thee, Cicely. They will be breaking in anon; and listen how they are screeching like wild cats."

"Oh! it is terrible," Cicely exclaimed; "and what if they get in and tear Mistress Kelly to pieces? Nay, I cannot desert her."

But Cicely found retreat impossible, the frightened people were pressing behind her, and the meek apprentice who kept guard in the shop, opened the door to let the struggling crowd pass out. Far away in the distance a clear voice was heard:

"You are cravens and fools as well, you will pay dear for this; but do you think you can stop the Lord's work?" Loud shrieks drowned her voice; and Will Purdy raising Cicely in his strong arms carried her beyond the reach of the tumult, and finally set her down within a few yards of Thomas Standfast's house.

She was a 'womanly woman,' and her legs were trembling and her breath coming in short hurried gasps, as she leaned for support against Will Purdy.

"I heard rumours that there was to be a great tumult, and they will never cease till they have silenced that woman's tongue. The man was not amiss, but I love not to hear women holding forth; they do say poor Master Kelly had need of the ducking-stool at times, and many a less ranting scold has had her tongue quieted down by the river yonder. Come now, say, 'Thank you, Will,'" the young man continued, "and say you'll give me a reward, eh? A kiss, Cicely, just one." But Cicely drew back.

"Ah! do not take advantage of me, Will Purdy; it is unmanly, it is cruel. I am so tired," and poor Cicely burst into tears.

"Tut, tut, sweet one, do but give me this reward, and I'll say no more, I'll bide my time." And then the heavy oaken door was thrown back by the watchman, and Cicely had soon scaled the wide staircase, and disappeared.

While the tumult and angry outcry of the rough Bristol people against the worshippers at Mistress Kelly's was going on, the baby whose christening feast had been celebrated that day, was sleeping peacefully on his mother's knee. Like all young mothers (worthy of that sacred name), Mistress Sarah Colston's thoughts went beyond the present moment, and took flight to the future, when the baby should be a boy and the boy grown into a man, doing his part in the great battle-field of life. Sarah Colston was glad to be alone after the excitement of the day, and glad to have her child all to herself. She was far from strong, and the decree had gone forth from the grandmother of the child that he was to be sent to a cottage on his father's estate at Winterbourne to be nursed. This weighed heavily on his mother's heart. She grudged to lose the companionship of her first-born in his days of awakening intelligence, and she was meditating how she could best resist carrying out the plan of banishment.

"Even Mistress Standfast is permitted to keep her babe with her; why should I be left without mine?" she said, looking up at her husband, who came to feast his eyes also on his son in the chamber appropriated to his wife's use.

"William, let me keep my treasure. Do not say he must go from me."

"Sweetheart," was the answer, "babies never thrive as well in the city as in the country. Thy mother lost three boys in succession. My mother mourned for one, and the mortality amongst the little ones is high. The child is but going to his own place, and there can be no nurse better for him than Joan Jennings at the farm. The boy will thrive on new milk drawn from the cow, and thou shalt visit him often on the new pillion which has been made soft and easy for thy use. New milk, methinks, as spring comes on, will put roses in thy pale cheeks.

"I will e'en be obedient, William," was the answer. "God has been very good to us, and I would fain be submissive to thy will—seeing His in it."

"I knew it, sweetheart," the husband said, touching the clenched fist of the boy, which was just visible outside his numerous wraps. "Thou art ever ready to submit, and I trust mine is not a heavy yoke. The boy will learn well from thee this grand lesson of life. There are signs of coming trouble, and it will go hard with those who try to keep their allegiance to the king whole and firm. There is much talk in our city concerning this ship money and much concerning the increase of pomp and magnificence in the Church, which those in high places are trying to force on the people. It will just drive moderate men to the extreme of lawlessness in matters of religion, and it will make the really loyal sons of the Church uneasy and suspicious; for, verily, we do not desire to throw ourselves again into the Pope's arms, and be slaves instead of freemen. Thy boy, if God spare his life, will see many great changes, and we must pray for him that he may be kept stedfast."

Here, as if in answer to his father's words,

the baby moved, and opening his eyes, smiled up at his mother.

"A real smile, William, see!" as the little mouth formed itself into the 'three-cornered smile' of early infancy. "Methinks he must know we speak of him; and see how fast he

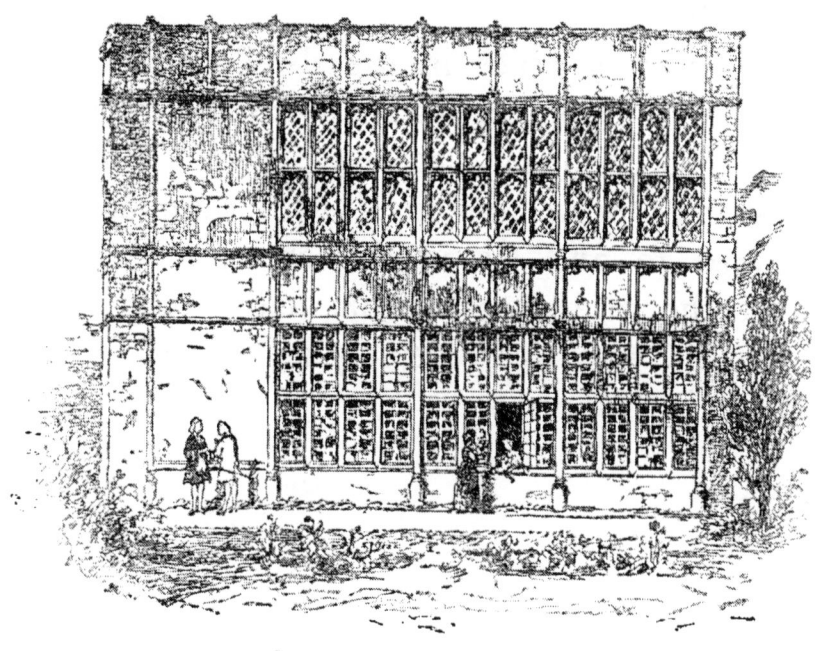

COLSTON'S HOUSE IN SMALL STREET

clutches thy finger. That is a good token of stedfastness, and the smile of benevolence. He will tread in thy steps, dear husband, and never turn his face away from any poor man."

Thus pleasing herself as she dwelt on the character of the babe on her knee, Mistress Colston forgot the trouble of parting from him —forgot the signs of tumult and rebellion of which her husband spoke, and, tired with the festivities of the day, soon after lay down to rest.

There was peace in the dwelling in Small Street, and the lot had apparently fallen to Sarah Colston in pleasant places. But her husband's brow was lined with care, and he walked to and fro in the chamber thinking over the grievances of his native city, long after his wife was sleeping as quietly as the infant in her arms.

THE GREAT HOUSE ON THE BRIDGE.

LITTLE Damaris Standfast, accompanied by Cicely bearing the muffled-up form of Baby Margery, left St. Mary le Port Street early in the bright December morning which followed the baptism feast of William Colston's first-born son.

The sun was shining brightly, and the old serving-man, who acted as watchman to the premises by night, and was Jack-of-all-trades by day for business and household requirements, preceded them, clearing the way and guiding little Mistress Damaris across the pitfalls of open sewers and ashpits which might lie in her path.

Damaris and her baby-sister were first to pay a visit to the baby in Small Street, and then proceed to the Great House at the Bridge End, where my Lady Rogers—being childless—loved to gather at times the children of her friends and neighbours in the city. Damaris was in great spirits. This day's pleasure would atone for the previous day's dullness.

"Not that I care for the baby," she said confidentially to old Peter, "but I would fain see the relics of the feast and the sweet gifts the god-parents gave; and I would fain have more of the cake. If I get it, I will give thee a good snack of it, Peter."

"You are always full of your promises, Mistress Damaris. They don't often come to much. Have a care!" for they now came by the High Cross, on a crowd surrounding some poor ragged men and boys, who were being taken off to the guard-room at the Castle on a charge of disturbing the public peace in High Street the night before. "They'll catch it; for Mistress Dorothy is not one to let her cause suffer. They do say there's them in the Council-chamber are on her side, and t'others, out of spite, will wink at all her smashed windows and egg-stained bodice. Poor creatures! they are more boys than men, and it's too bad to put 'em in stinking dungeons."

Damaris's large wistful eyes followed the crowd, and at this moment Robert Haynes, the writing-master, came up, and said to Cicely, "You were soon flown yesternight, Mistress Cicely. Afore the blow fell you were off. Well, well," he added, with a sly twinkle in his eye, "it's good to have a lover to hand at a pinch. It was worth some toil and pains to hear that young scholar hold forth. Why, since we lost our godly Mr. Yeamans we have had nought like it. He can speak to the heart; but these poor fellows know not at what they scoff; and I cannot abide seeing them shut up in Newgate."

As the crowd moved on Peter and his charges crossed to Small Street, and here, in a stately hall, they found two serving-men, who conducted Damaris and Cicely with little Margery to the beautiful dining-hall, where the remains of yesterday's feast were arranged on the board for dinner at noon.

Damaris gazed with child-like delight on the pasties richly ornamented with figures of the animals which had furnished their contents. Here was a pullet with a scarlet comb, and here a rabbit with heels in the air, and pink comfits for its eyes. Then there were innumerable sweet dishes of comfitures and preserves, made of rich West Indian fruit; while the oranges of Seville, and the dried grapes from Malaga were served in various ways.

The great chrisom cake stood in the middle of the board, and was ornamented with a *fac-*

simile in sugar of the Temple Church, with its leaning tower, where Edward Colston had been

THE TEMPLE CHURCH.

baptised. Then there were the large silver flagons, and the grace cup, at the head of the board, which had been passed round so freely the day before, as the health of the baby was drunk. It seemed hard to believe that some twenty people had partaken of the viands only yesterday, so much was left.

Master William Colston came from a small room opening out of the dining-hall, and greeted Damaris kindly. He took a little silver box from the glittering heap of plate on the great sideboard, and filling it with a handful of dry sweets, said—

"Here, keep this token in memory of my son's christening day."

"For my very own! Oh! how good you are!" Damaris exclaimed; "and are all these the christening gifts? Look! Cicely, at these spoons," but Cicely answered demurely, "Methinks I would rather see the babe, an' it please you, than these worldly gauds which ill suit the occasion."

William Colston gave Cicely a stern glance from his deep-set eyes, and a sharp rebuke rose to his lips; but the sweet face, tinged with rose colour, which so calmly met his, seemed to soften him, he hardly knew why.

"Well, well, go up to my wife's chamber. You will show the way," he added, turning to a servant, "and take Master Standfast's serving-man to the buttery. I must e'en be at the Council-chamber for an hour before I dine."

"Master Colston," Damaris said, catching hold of the velvet cape which the rich merchant wore, clasped with a heavy silver clasp at the throat, "Master Colston, prythee look at our baby Margery."

As Cicely held the child up to William Colston, she stretched out her hand to reach the silver clasp.

"A pretty little maiden," he said. "I shall be right glad when our Edward is grown to that age. She must be some months old."

"Ten months come Christmas Day," Cicely said. "But she is forward for that age, and has great understanding."

William Colston looked at Baby Margery as men are wont to look at a baby, as something of a natural curiosity, and then calling the servant who attended him to the Council-chamber, he was gone.

Damaris held her precious silver box in one hand, and in the other a huge wedge of the christening cake and one of the ornaments from the Boar's head, which she prized almost more than her other treasures.

At the top of the wide stairs she stopped,

looking back at Cicely, who was ascending more slowly with Margery in her arms. As Damaris turned, a ray of wintry sunshine caught the silver box, and Margery held out her hands towards it, as she had done for the silver clasp on William Colston's cloak.

"As if I would give thee that," Damaris said. "Nay, nay, not I. Thou canst not have all my precious things, though Cicely would give thee the moon, an' she could."

"All my precious things!" The words were remembered in after years, and took a deeper meaning than Damaris then could dream of.

Mistress Colston was seated by the fire with her boy on her knee. She was evidently a mother of another type than Mistress Standfast.

There were servants enough and to spare in William Colston's household, but little Edward's mother grudged to give him up to any hands but hers, till the sad day came when he must go to Winterbourne.

"Ah! Damaris Standfast," she said, looking up with a bright smile, "I am right glad you are come; and Cicely Knight and the Baby Margery. I bid you welcome. Bring hither your baby and let her see mine."

Damaris advanced cautiously to the tiny six-weeks-old baby, and looked down curiously at its face. She was apparently fascinated by it, and murmured,

"He is very fair to look on. I love him," bending down to kiss all that was visible of the child's face.

Then Cicely drew near with Margery in her arms. Margery drew back as if doubtful at first. A great gulf seemed set between that tiny babe of a few weeks and her superior ten months!

But Cicely gently let her down on a level with the little Edward, and then she smiled, and her hand touched his face as if to make an overture of friendship.

"Dear babes," exclaimed Mistress Colston; "they are a sweet pair."

"Nay, not a pair," said Damaris, with her ever-ready tongue, "for one is bigger and older than the other by ten months. They are no pair."

"Damaris," Cicely said, reprovingly, "it is not meet to contradict thy elders and betters; fie! for shame."

Mistress Colston only smiled and said,

"There is truth in what thou sayest, Damaris; but there may be two meanings to the word pair. I hope Master Colston showed thee all the christening ornaments; but didst thou take note of the cloth on which they were spread. If not, I will descend and show it to thee and Cicely, for it will be folded and laid by with the heirlooms of the Colstons after to-day, when my husband will bring some friends from the Council-chamber to dine at noon."

Mistress Colston delivered the baby to the nurse who was in waiting, with a kiss and low-spoken "the Lord bless thee;" and then, taking Damaris by the hand, she led her down once more to the great hall.

"See," she said, "the great-grandsire of our babe entertained the Queen Elizabeth in the year of grace 1574, one hundred and two years ago. This cloth was used at the banquet, and it is rare and beautiful. Stand here, Damaris, and look down the board. There is the great queen on horseback, so life-like, wove into the damask. See, the eyes in the peacocks' tails, and the great lilies and roses so well formed. And there is a boar hunt at this end, and other sports."

"It is a brave cloth," Damaris said, musing, "and you are grand folks to entertain a queen. His present Majesty may come hither, and then, Mistress Colston, wilt thou let me see him? I would be ever so quiet and good, for I *would* like to see the king."

"The king has no thought that I know of of visiting Bristol," Mistress Colston said; "but I will think of you, Damaris, if ever such a great honour is mine, as to receive his sacred person."

"Sacred!" murmured Cicely Knight, "methinks there is naught that is sacred or holy in a king or prince more than in common folk."

Mistress Colston took no heed of Cicely's remark, and after a goodly supply of more comfits and ornaments, as many as the deep pockets in Cicely's and Damaris's gowns could hold, Peter was summoned by one of the servants, and Damaris, springing towards him, exclaimed, "See, Peter, what treasures! Put them all in thy leather pouch, all but the silver box. I will keep that myself; and, Peter, you shall have two snacks of cake, and a real Seville orange, and—"

"My Lady Rogers will be angered if we are late," Cicely said; "we must delay no longer, Damaris."

Damaris made a grimace, and said, "I do not greatly love my Lady Rogers and all her dull talk. I have enow of that from yourself,

Cicely. But I like to watch the craft on the river, and the foreign sailors with their bright caps."

Damaris and Cicely, with the baby, now bent their steps towards the bridge, which was a narrow thoroughfare and always crowded.

At this time of day, between eleven and twelve, the business was at its height, and there was a brisk trade carried on in the mercers' stores, whose gay stuffs of foreign manufacture hung like banners, and gained more attention than the cloths and taffetas made nearer home.

The spice merchants and fruiterers were in great request at this season, when in every house there were preparations for the feast of Christmas, except, indeed, in the houses of the strict Puritans, who were beginning to hold all observance of what they deemed the 'mass' as godless, though only the extreme members of their party took extreme measures like Mistress Dorothy Kelly. Little Damaris Standfast was lifted in old Peter's arms that she might have a better view of the stores and shops over the heads of the throng of buyers and sellers.

"See, Peter! what a lot of gold stuff! how it glitters and glistens! I should love to have it. And see that strange clock at the clockmaker's! They are winding it up; and there comes the cock out to crow, and the Apostle Peter—what a red comb he hath!"

"The Apostle or the cock?" said a voice near. "Come away, Damaris Standfast, nor stand gazing on such folly."

The reproving voice came from a tall buxom woman, the wife of Richard Vickers, and well known as one of the leaders of the feminine band of stout-hearted Puritans.

"Move on with the child," she said, addressing Peter; "and come, Cicely Knight, thou hast hard work to press through this throng of worldly self-seekers with that babe. Methinks she, at least, would be best in her cradle or on her mother's knee."

"An' it please you, Mistress Vickers, we are bidden to the great house at t'other end of the bridge to my Lady Rogers."

"I am bound thither also; but follow me, and I'll clear the way, I warrant."

The good lady passed on, elbowing and pushing past the most attractive stores, and Damaris, from her post of observation in Peter's arms, laughed to see her.

"A great fuss she makes, forsooth. Oh! Peter, let me see that rare bird with colours on its breast. Cicely, Cicely! see yon bird; is it sinful to be decked out in crimson and purple? I warrant you think the brown sparrows and throstles in Bullock's Park have the best of it."

But Cicely made no reply; she was only anxious to follow her guide to a less crowded part of the bridge. They passed now under the arched gateway above which the chapel, used as a store-house, was raised. But little remained of the internal beauty of that chapel; but without, the large mullioned windows caught the sun's noon-day rays, and the tower reared its head proudly to the pale blue of the wintry sky.

The Mayor and Aldermen of the old city assembled in a vaulted chamber of good workmanship beneath, and the religious element had died out from the beautiful structure at the time of the dissolution of the monasteries in the last century.

Mistress Vickers always felt a thrill of horror as she passed under the chapel archway, and she gave vent to her feelings now by saying,

"There is need to raise one's voice for the truth, or verily we'll have the priests mumbling out of the mass-book again, and dressing up like mountebanks in the chapel, and puffing the incense like to choke one. Better by far pull down every stick and stone of the place—nay, burn it with fire—than that."

The further part of the bridge was not so crowded, and a scrivener, and barber-surgeon, with a long pole sticking out from the middle story, did not attract so many customers.

At the scrivener's door, indeed, stood two women patiently waiting their turn to pass into the room beyond the front shop, where a clerk sat, to get a letter written to an absent son, who was in Spain in an office there.

A chance had offered for the transmission of the letter by one of the ships in the docks, and the mother and betrothed maiden took the opportunity of writing to the absent one. For a small fee the master scrivener would write the words which neither mother nor maiden could transcribe for themselves; writing being taught to very few of the lower middle class in those days.

From the barber-surgeon's house a poor man was just issuing, with a white face and tottering step, leaning on the arm of his wife. He had just lost a pint of blood from his arm, and had paid a fee in proportion, to the man whose trade it was to take the life-blood of sick people, and hasten them to their graves. Men of law had also their houses at this end of the bridge. A brother of Mistress Colston, Humphrey Batten, whose father was a barrister in Temple Street, transacted legal business here for him—such as the transfer of deeds, and other matters.

At last the party reached the stately mansion, which it is hard for us to realise now-a-days.

It is described as vast in proportions and with a lofty lantern tower rising in the centre.

The great hall was of tesselated marble, supported on pillars, and here were several servants with the badge of the Rogers family on their sleeves.

The staircase of oak was elaborately carved, and of several flights, separating mid-way to the right and left.

Mistress Vickers apparently knew her way well, and turned to the left of the grand staircase, puffing and blowing and perfectly at home. A curtain of old arras hung over a door, at which Mistress Vickers tapped, and it was opened by a plainly dressed waiting-maid, who was evidently one of the same community as Cicely, for a warm greeting passed between them.

"My lady is expecting you," she said; "and

the embroidery has been ready and the silks sorted for an hour past. She is just now in converse with Mistress Kelly, in the inner chamber; but prythee sit down, Cicely, and I will fetch the babe some warm draught, poor babe!" for little Margery was evidently weary of her lengthened perambulation, and, sweet-tempered as she was, began to cry.

"Hush, hush! my sweetheart," Cicely said, sinking into a chair, while Mrs. Vickers passed, in the confidence of an intimate friend, into the inner chamber, whence came the sound of a woman's voice in prayer. "Hush, sweetheart! I must take thee home, for it ill suits thee to be on the move for hours together." Meanwhile Damaris had gone to her favourite station in one of the latticed windows which, unlike those in her own home, commanded an extensive view of the river and of the ships, while beyond were the wooded heights of Kingsdown and the rocky, uneven, steep hills, which are now cut out in many streets and terraces.

Damaris now and then unscrewed the top of her silver comfit box, and tasted one of the sweets within it. She did not care for Lady Rogers' lessons in needlework and her long exhortations on the duty of children to their elders, but she loved inexpressibly to gaze out on that river, and watch the ships, and ponder whence they came and whither they were going.

Damaris's young soul was awaking to the consciousness of a world wider than that city of Bristol where, so it seemed to her, the thoughts and interests of everyone connected with her were centred; a world toward which that solemn-looking river flowed to the wide sea, across which so many sailed and brought back treasures and riches. If only she could go thither and be rocked to sleep by the curtseying of the boat on the waves, what joy it would be! How delightful to have the wide canopy of heaven above her, to see the clouds sail from east to west, instead of catching scant glimpses of them between the overhanging roofs of Mary le Port Street.

Even here in Lady Rogers' grand house there were the closely packed roofs of the Bridge Street to intercept the view in one direction; but to her delight a flight of seagulls were swooping down on the river, their wings shining like burnished silver in the rays of the wintry sun.

"Beautiful birds! I wish I were a bird and

could fly like them. Cicely, dost thou see the gulls?"

"They are signs of storms," said a demure little waiting-maid, who had brought the hot drink for the baby Margery. "They always come up at low tide before a storm, seeking the small fish and eels in the mud. Last night's sunset told of a storm; the heavens were flaming, and there was a great sword hung right over the Cathedral. They said it was a token of God's judgment falling on it."

"Did you see the sword?" Damaris asked, her dark eyes glistening.

"Yes, and a dragon with a fiery tail in a green sea," replied the maid, colouring her picture to suit her listener's eager wonder. "My lady says that the sky foretold the vengeance of the Lord on this city."

"But, Amice, sure the sky hangs over the sea; and other parts besides Bristol; why should the token be for this city only?"

"I cannot tell," was the answer; "but my lady saith so. It betokened anger."

"I saw some rose-coloured clouds," said Damaris; "they looked like love and kindness, not anger. But it is all fable. I am getting hungry; when will dinner be served?"

"It is not quite twelve of the clock; it will be served at twelve. My lady is giving counsel to Mistress Kelly; and Mistress Vickers is come to help to settle the weighty matters concerning the riot at the meeting, and the disturbance of the godly Master Hassard and his ministration. Perchance he will remain here in the room of Master Yeamans, if the Lord will; and it will be a blessing for His people."

The consultation was over at length, and Mistress Kelly departed, nodding to Cicely as she passed her, but saying nothing. The bond of a common faith was very strong amongst the women of the time, and Lady Rogers warmly supported the movement of independence in worship, and the stout resistance against the upholders of the High Church party. But for all that, there was a gulf set, between my Lady Rogers of the Bridge House, and Dorothy Kelly, the grocer of High Street!

Lady Rogers had bidden Mistress Vickers to dinner, but she had only offered Mistress Kelly a glass of mead and canary wine, and some sweet cakes, thereby showing a distinction!

Now the little lady came over to Damaris and said she supposed she would like to eat before work, patted her cheek asked how her good father was, and then examined Margery with a critical air—not a maternal air, for Lady Rogers was childless.

"She favours her mother," exclaimed Mistress Vickers, "and looks a child born for the high places of kings' palaces, and fine clothes."

"Ah!" said Lady Rogers, casting up her eyes, "that is a poor look-out for sinful creatures whom it ill becomes to dress up in gauds and finery when the cause of the Lord lieth in the dust."

How it was that the fair child lying so peacefully in Cicely's arms should evoke this apostrophe it seems hard to understand, and it did not come with particularly good grace from Lady Rogers, who lived in one of the most princely houses in old Bristol.

The part of a 'mother in Israel' had been with one consent conferred on Lady Rogers, and all matters connected with 'the faithful' were referred to her.

As soon as the mid-day meal was over, Cicely and her charge were sent home under the care of one of Lady Rogers' numerous retainers, while Damaris was summoned to her work in a small chamber with two of the projecting windows I have described, at the side of the house abutting on the river.

Lady Rogers and Mistress Vickers had much to say to each other that afternoon, so that Damaris was left very much to the care of Amice to pursue her needle craft.

Poor child! this task was the penalty paid for visits to the Great House at the Bridge End, and she was particularly disinclined for it after her morning's dissipation. She pricked her finger and knotted her silks, and whispered to Amice that 'the peacock' was right down ugly which she was supposed to copy in fine tapestry stitch.

"And of what use is it, Amice?" she asked.

"All gentlewomen ought to learn to use their needles."

"Mother is of higher degree than we are," said Damaris, "and she never takes a needle unless it is to string beads for the edge of her cap, or twist gold thread into devices for her bodice."

Amice was silent. She did not like to say what was in her heart, that Mistress Margaret Standfast did not lead a very useful or active life.

The appointed task was over at last, and then, having finished her talk with Mistress

Vickers, Lady Rogers bid Damaris draw near and read to her from the Gospels.

The people of England were justly proud at this time of their lately authorized version of the Bible, with the grandiloquent address to 'that high and mighty King James.'

As Damaris took the book she turned back to the first page and saw that the preface was gone. Lady Rogers had cut it out as profane.

Damaris always liked to read the first line, as it seemed to place the Book and the people alike under the shadow of royalty!

"Who has taken away the first page, my Lady?" she asked. "There is no word of the King's Majesty."

"There is no need," was the reply. "We need no title of an earthly monarch to stare us in the face, as we draw nigh the Word of the King of kings."

"I liked to see it," Damaris almost sighed; "and the big letters and flourish—"

"Open at the place I tell thee, nor waste time over such idle fancies."

Damaris did as she was bid, and read with tolerable ease the first few verses of the seventh chapter of the Gospel of St. Matthew:—
"Judge not, that ye be not judged. For with

what judgment ye mete it shall be measured to you again." When Damaris had ended, she looked up at Lady Rogers and said—

"Did you think that the fiery dragon yester even, my Lady, boded judgments? What judgments?"

"Alas, child, I cannot say! but that God will avenge His own speedily, I doubt not. Here, in this city of Bristol, there are crowds of ungodly folks, and the shepherds in the Church are blind leaders of the blind. Our sins are truly great. A popish princess sharing the king's throne; the people forced back to the thraldom of the papacy; misrule and riot going hand-in-hand. Nay, child, the flaming sword hung over Bristol had a meaning, I doubt not. I would, child, that thou hadst more teaching at thy own home, but the Lord is forgotten there."

"Nay, now nay," said little Damaris. "My father is as godly a man as lives, and Cicely Knight talks after your fashion, my Lady, and mother keeps her church on Sunday, though not on Feast days and the Saints' days, as Mistress Colston doth."

"The Colstons may not be taken as an example, child. They are brimful of the world and follow not the paths of peace."

Mistress Vickers, who had been dozing in her chair, now roused herself, and said it was time she was departing, and she would see Damaris home.

But this intention was not carried out, as Master Standfast was announced by a serving-man to be in waiting for his little girl.

Damaris sprang to Amice, and begged her to help her to put on her hood and cloak, and then making Lady Rogers a deep curtsey, she kissed her hand, and with a much slighter reverence to Mistress Vickers, she was gone.

It was delightful to get to the Great House, but it was also delightful to get away, and a walk with her father was indeed a treat. These two had so much in common, for Thomas Standfast had a great deal of that imaginative element which was the sunbeam of his little daughter's life. Damaris related the events of the day, beginning at the mansion in Small Street, the lately-christened baby, and the grand silver plate. Then of her passage along the crowded thoroughfare on Peter's shoulders, and of the long waiting for dinner at the Great House on the bridge.

Thomas Standfast listened and made rejoinders which showed he listened, and the traffic of the wheels being much lessened, he led his little daughter round by St. Augustine's Back, and crossed thence to the Bullock's Park by College Green.

The western sky was clear in the evening light, a crescent moon hung in it, just above the tower of the Cathedral, but there was no flaming sword or dragon's tail in the heavens to-night.

All was clear and bright, but with no vivid colours.

"Father," said little Damaris, "do you think very dreadful times are at hand for the city? Amice saith that the flaming sword held over Bristol, meant woe and danger."

"Tut-tut! my little one. The Almighty does not write His judgments in the colours of the heavens. But I will not say, Damaris, that I think the times are like to be peaceable. There is a spirit abroad everywhere, which tells of faction and rebellion. And there are some in this city, who would be in the forefront of the rebels, if it comes to that. Albeit they are as quiet as foxes in their holes: they are burrowing deep; and the Council-chamber, where we ought to meet only with true and loyal servants of the king, is not free of these sly perverters of the truth. But thou art too young for talk like this, child. See, we are turning towards Mary le Port, and I must away to my business—for I hear the good ship *Elizabeth* is in port, from Lisbon."

Father and daughter turned into the darkness of the overhanging houses of Mary le Port Street, there vanishing from our sight in the gloom and shadows. Much will come and go before we see Damaris Standfast again; and the old city of Bristol will have gone through the changes and chances of war and pestilence more terrible than any flaming sword in the sunset sky of Edward Colston's christening feast day.

But when night closed in over the city streets, and the busy concourse of the day was over, a mother knelt by the cradle of her first-born son, and prayed that the God and Father to whom he had been dedicated in baptism, would bless the lad, and 'grant that he might lead the rest of his life according to that beginning.'

A mother's prayer shall bring an answer of peace, beyond the stormy days which lay between this night and that distant time, when the voices of the children in the dim future, should be raised to call her boy blessed.

BOOK II.

FORECASTS.

"'Tis but an hour ago since it was nine,
  And after one hour more 'twill be eleven
And so from hour to hour we ripe and ripe,
  And thereby hangs a tale."

Shakespeare.

BOOK II

JUNE, 1657.

SUMMER DAYS.

"Damaris, it is a full hour since you have uttered a word. Methinks it is a dull and dreary life enow for me, anyhow; and methinks too you might enliven it, and not sit scraping that pen on the rough paper till I feel fit to rush at it and tear it to fragments. Damaris!"

"Well-a-day, Margery, find thy own employment, nor grudge me mine. I like to study and write, and then—"

"I like to dance and sing and be merry," Margery exclaimed, throwing down her embroidery frame. "Was ever a maiden so moped as I am? I shall be off to Spain in the next ship that sails, and you'll see me no more. But in sober earnest, Damaris, we are in a sorry plight, with a sick mother, who does not know black from white, and only speaks to wail; and though the Purdys are excellent folk, and I love Cicely, they are but dull, and father is more silent every day, and frowns if we say we want to be merry. I am sick of it, and no wonder."

"Do not be so ill-contented, Margery. I am sure Mistress Colston is a good friend, and many is the time she has made us welcome in Small Street."

"All the world seems asleep, and the Bristol folks are too money-loving to be gay. I wish the Lord Protector were sent beyond the seas instead of our lawful King Charles. I warrant he would soon tell these cross-grained people of Bristol to dance round the Maypole and drink the spiced bowl, and bring back the pageant, and—but who is coming? I hear a footstep." And Margery sprang to her feet.

The room in Mary le Port Street had changed but little in these twenty years; people did not refurnish their rooms continually in those days. Except that the old tapestry had been renewed by an embroidered curtain, the work of Damaris and her maidens, there was but little alteration since the December afternoon when Margery lay an infant in Cicely's arms, and Damaris stood at the casement watching for the return of her parents from Edward Colston's christening feast. Margery had grown up into a beautiful young woman. She had something of the patrician in her air and bearing, but, in spite of a natural gaiety and sprightliness, she had more depth of character than her poor mother, now a helpless, paralyzed invalid, whose beauty and charm of voice and manner were but a dream of the past.

But many eyes turned from Margery to her elder sister, just as we turn from the gay beauty of a flower-bed to rest our eyes on the cool shaven turf lying round some old cathedral, with a sense of relief.

As the two sisters stood together with eyes directed to the door, when a knock was heard, they formed a contrast such as I have described. Damaris was thirty, it is true, and ten years separated her from the brilliant and youthful Margery; but Damaris was in the very prime of womanhood, and there was in her face a certain attraction which it is not easy to put into words.

It was the shining of the soul through the eyes, and the sweet curves which the law of kindness wreathed round her mouth; it was the womanly womanliness of every movement which was so fascinating to those who had eyes to see it.

In these days Damaris Standfast would have been called a woman of culture and refinement. She would probably have made her mark by some administrative power in an intellectual or philanthropic centre. But women in the year of grace 1657 had to find their own level, and had but few external helps. Damaris, it is true, had seen enough passing before her eyes in these twenty years to awake in her mind keen interest, not unmixed with sorrow and wonder, in the events of her native city. And in a reflective mind like hers, many grave thoughts were stirring. It had been said that with the Roman Faith, benevolence and ministering to the sick and afflicted had died out. That the care of the poor was forgotten by the Reformed Church in England, and that with the dissolution and destruction of the monasteries the spirit of Christian charity had utterly vanished!

Damaris Standfast, in a small circle, was daily proving that some hearts at least recognised the breadth and length and height of Christian love; and wherever it was possible she dropped the balm of Gilead into wounds of body and soul. Her father had many people in his employment, and, unlike the sons and daughters of the wealthy merchants generally, she held herself responsible for their welfare. Many a care was confided to Mistress Damaris many a sad heart comforted, many a dying bed watched over, with sympathy and tenderness. The entire absence of all Puritanic dress, voice, and gesture, made her a most valuable defender of the faith, which holds, that the loving Father of us all takes no pleasure in the self-imposed penalties and austerities of His children. How it was that the child whom we saw borne aloft in old Peter's arms to the Bridge House, full of eager delight with the spoils she had gathered after Edward Colston's christening feast, and who resented the admonitions of Lady Rogers and Dorothy Kelly with impatience ; how it was that the child had developed into the gracious and beautiful woman, far in advance of her day and generation, I cannot say. But that these troublous days of anarchy and confusion did produce such women, in various ranks and degrees, is true ; and, if rare, the more striking was their appearance as, like flowers by the wayside, they dispensed beauty and fragrance in their city or neighbourhood.

As Damaris stood with her arms thrown round Margery, with expectant eyes fastened on the door, it opened slowly, and a tall young man, dressed after the fashion of the day, with long heavy rolls of hair lying on his shoulders, advanced to the two girls.

Both looked at him with a puzzled expression. Young gallants did not often mount those wide, dark stairs. Margery's beauty had been, as she complained, doomed to blush unseen in the shadows of St. Mary le Port Street.

The gentleman held his plumed cap in his hand, and bowing somewhat stiffly, said:

"I have an errand from my mother, Mistress Colston. She prays that Master Standfast's daughters will sup with her in Small Street at six of the clock, and that the evening being warm and the light prolonged, they will join her in repairing to the park to hear the birds singing. You do not call me to mind, Mistress Damaris?"

"Yes," Damaris said: "sure it is Master Edward Colston."

"At your service," was the quick rejoinder. "Has Mistress Margery forgotten me?"

"No," said Margery, "I mind me now: you came hither last when he they now call Lord

Protector was taking ship to Ireland. Who will say I have not a long memory?"

"When pricked to wake up," Damaris said, "but sure you were but a child then."

"I remember Master Edward Colston was a boy, if I was a child," Margery said with a toss of her pretty head, which recalled her mother in days past. "I called him, in my mind, the boy that never smiled, and said to Cicely he ought to come to her meeting-house; and even now he hath a look which I see in Master Hassard's face when he rebuketh me for love of the world. Master Colston would fain rebuke me also, an' he could get a hearing. Perchance he may get one this evening in the Park; but I would as lieve hear the nightingale's song as any one preach!"

"I would leave the preaching to the rightful clergy," said Edward Colston. "I have no mind to cast in my lot with the Puritan or Quaker."

"You look little indeed like either," said Margery, with a silvery laugh. "Would you not fain read all those sheets of yellow paper at which Damaris sits and scribbles hour after hour? I saw your name written there, Master Edward Colston."

"Hush, Margery," said her sister; "do not

be such a chatterbox. We must," said she, turning to Edward Colston, "all find our pastime in what pleases us most. I have long ago made notes of what has happened, and verily there are dark places indeed, as I look back on the last twenty years."

And now the patter of little feet was heard on the stairs, and a servant ushered into the room half-a-dozen children, in the garb of men and women; plainly dressed Puritan children, who had each a bag; the two boys had a lesson book and a Testament, the girls needlework.

"These are Damaris's children; she teaches them the Catechism, and hears them read, and—"

"Whose children are they?" Edward Colston asked.

"They are the children of our good friend and servant, Cicely Purdy, who married my father's apprentice some years agone. That is to say, four are her children, and the others are picked up when Damaris goes for her walks in the city. She teaches them because she likes it; as for me, I'd box their ears, and lay a whip on their backs every minute, if I had the teaching of them."

Edward Colston laughed.

"The children would soon rebel, methinks. But, Mistress Damaris, it is a fine thought of yours to teach the little ones. It is a work worthy of a Bristol gentlewoman. I will not detain you longer, as we shall meet anon," he added in a low voice, as he parted from the sisters with a bow, and bending one knee with a certain formal grace, which was remarkable in so young a man.

"He might be as old as our father in manners, and yet he is handsome. Didst notice his love-lock, Damaris? He must have been in a good set in London. I wonder that some Roundhead has not cut it off—on the sly; but now I must go and look out our garments. I shall don my white sarcenet, and the velvet bodice with the lace apron, and my hood with cherry ribbons."

Damaris, who was seating herself before her little scholars, said, "Go, and visit mother in her chamber, and tell her of Edward Colston."

Margery shrugged her shoulders, and murmured, "I must think of my dress first."

"Alas, poor child! always dress and self first," sighed Damaris.

Meantime Edward Colston walked away,

first greeting Master Standfast, who was crossing the hall.

Thomas Standfast had aged much in these years. He had grown prematurely old, and he wore a heavy wig, which made his face look thinner and more pinched than it might otherwise have done.

"Ah! Master," he said, looking curiously at the young man, "what is it I can do for you? The days are none of the brightest now in the trade of Bristol; but step into my chamber."

"Thanks, good sir. I come only to pay my respectful duty to my father's old friend. I have been absent from Bristol for years, and am like to be absent again."

Then seeing Thomas Standfast still looked puzzled, he said,

"Edward Colston, at your service."

"And I am right glad to see you, young sir. I prythee take supper with us this evening."

"Nay, I have come to bid you to our house in Small Street. Your daughters have promised their company, and my mother will be honoured by yours."

"I may look in perchance, by your leave, and escort my girls back; but I have much pressing at this time. What says your good father as to Cromwell's inauguration at Westminster?"

"He saith," said Edward Colston, "that the power of the tyrant will decline an' he flaunts it before the eyes of the country. The Crown next, and then, perchance, the axe."

"Aye, verily, that is well spoken. There's but few left in this city loyal and true. I'm an old man, but I may yet live to see these traitors punished."

"Forsooth, Master Standfast," said a man dressed in the very extreme of the Puritan fashion, in a coarse cloth dress, very plain and buttoned close to the throat, with a pointed collar, and cuffs of the long coat turned back; "forsooth, this youngster is over-bold, and had best learn discretion."

"Tut-tut! Purdy. This is Master Edward Colston."

Will Purdy, thus transformed from the gay, rollicking apprentice of the past, had risen to be a person of great importance in Thomas Standfast's business. He had been converted to Puritan views by the preaching of the young minister, Master Hassard, who had married the valiant widow, Dorothy Kelly, and had been her meek and dutiful coadjutor for many years. Will Purdy was a man on whom fortune smiled. He had many private ventures of his own, and had scraped together a pretty little sum. But as he had once been careless and gay, given to oaths and drinking deep of every stoup of ale which came in his way, he was now precise and bigoted,—held strong opinions, adopted the true nasal twang, and talked glibly of the mercy which had snatched him from hell. That so sweet and winning a creature as Cicely Knight could marry him is one of the matrimonial enigmas I cannot attempt to solve. Probably, when she rejoiced in her gentle heart over him, as a brand plucked from the burning, pity, which is ever near akin to love, triumphed, and was quickened by her desire to keep the lost piece of silver bright and shining, as she believed, for the good of the Lord's people.

Will Purdy, in reply to Master Thomas Standfast's reproof, turned up his eyes, and said,

"A Colston, forsooth! we know well of what stock he comes then." And then Will Purdy, without a sign of respect for either his master and superior, or for young Edward Colston, passed into the room beyond.

"Poor Will! He hath scant manners," said

Thomas Standfast by way of apology. "He is a good and trusted servant and friend, nor would he see me wronged of a doit; but—well, well, it is best to hold our peace, but if ever the king has his own again, then we'll see a bit of time-service as before in this city of ours. I crave your pardon for detaining you so long here in the hall; but we will meet anon," and then Thomas Standfast turned to his room, and Edward Colston took his departure.

Edward Colston had been, as he said, absent from Bristol for the greater part of his boyhood and he had now returned to arrange with his father to carry on in Spain the commerce which was to lay the foundation of his princely fortune.

He was very grave and very old for his years. The young brothers and sisters in the Small Street mansion looked on him with some fear. He seemed so far apart from boyish pastimes and sports. His father's life had been a prosperous one in many ways, but a dark cloud rested over him as a true and stedfast Royalist. He had never flinched once from his duty to his king, and endured the reproaches of his companions in the Council-chamber, and his dismissal from the board, with composure and calm dignity. But no man who had passed through the changes and chances of those years lying between 1637 and 1657 could fail to bear the traces of what he had suffered in the sufferings of others. The home in Small Street would have been somewhat dull for those young brothers and sisters, who had succeeded Edward in the nursery, had it had not been for the bright and happy temper of the mother.

Mistress Colston had all the qualities which are necessary for a wife and mother. Thrifty, and looking well to the ways of her household, she was ever ready to enter into plans for their amusement, and many a time her brightness dispelled the clouds which would gather over the sky of home. All the children loved and trusted her; but between her first-born son and his mother, the tie was more than commonly strong.

He had been, as we know, sent away from her in his infancy. And for the greater part of his childhood and boyhood he had been separated from her. But when they did meet, it was a joy with which strangers could not intermeddle.

On his return from his errand in Mary le Port Street, Edward Colston found his mother in her own chamber, answering to the morning room of these times. The brightness of the summer morning seemed to shed a halo over her, as she sat with a hornbook on her knee, where a little maiden was spelling out a lesson with great pains; her mother, meanwhile, engaged with her needle, and keeping a watchful eye on William, her youngest boy, who was hacking a bit of wood into what he thought was a boat, in the recess of the wide window.

When Edward came into the room, little Mall, as she was called, clapped her hands.

"Prythee no more tasks, mother. Give me leave to go down to the still-room with Will, where Doll is making some sweetbreads with a paste of almonds. She said I might crack the shells."

"Mother, I'll go," said Will, jumping down from his elevation in the window-seat. And he was rushing out of the room when his brother called to him.

"See there, Will, you have overset the basket where mother keeps her balls of worsted; forget not good manners, Will, be the haste ever so great."

Will looked up defiantly at his elder brother, and said, "I'll pick them up for mother, not because you bid me."

As the boy was stooping over the basket with a red face, and murmuring some words which his mother did not wish to notice, Edward Colston took little Mall in his arms, and set her on his shoulder.

"Will you bring me some of the sweet cake, when it is baked, eh, Mall? and give me a kiss as a pledge?"

The child stroked her brother's handsome face, and said, "You great big brother, you seem like another father." And then she struggled to her feet without giving the kiss.

When the children were gone, Edward Colston's whole manner changed; he went up to his mother, and throwing himself on a bench by her side, said,

"I am but a stranger at home, dear mother, a stranger to all but thee. Let the younger boys bide here, it is better to live with one's kindred."

"Ah, dear son," said Mistress Colston, "thy father speaks of sending Thomas and Robert to Spain ere long, as well as thyself. The trade is extending its borders yearly, and he needs a Colston, he saith, wherever the trading is carried on in his name. But talk not of parting yet, dear son; let me feel that I have and hold you for a few short weeks. Tell me, didst see the two maidens in Mary le Port Street, and deliver my message?"

"Yes; and they will be right glad to come at thy bidding. Mother, is not Mistress Margery accounted a beauty?"

"Yes, indeed; and it is a marvel that she is yet unwed. But the poor children live a lonely life—the mother ailing and helpless, the father well on in years, and, like thy own dear father, Edward, showing signs of age. Ah, me! Doth thy father strike thee as greatly changed?"

"He is older in figure, and stoops more; but there is yet a fire in his eye which I never saw equalled. He is harder of hearing, perchance?"

"Ah, yes, yes; but do not notice it to him, Edward. Methinks if ever the king has his own, and this Council-chamber is purged of the fanatics, thy father will revive. He saith often that the murder of his Majesty and the sins of the people seem to press on him as his own. But let us speak of more cheerful matters. And as for me, am I not a proud wife, when I call to mind that since that day, now twelve years agone, when thy father wrapped his scarlet robe around him, and walked like a soldier to the fight, with the roll of the drum and the whistle of the fife piercing the air, he has never flinched or faltered. They banished him from the Council-chamber, and stripped him of his dignity; but 'Sweetheart,' he saith to me on his return, 'Skippon can do this, but he cannot banish me from a Higher Council-chamber, where I may plead amidst all my shortcomings, that I have "feared God and honoured my king."'"

Edward Colston watched his mother's face as she spoke, glowing with her wifely enthusiasm and pride, and exclaimed—

"Changes and chances have not left many marks on thee, sweet mother; so young you still look, and, in my eyes at least, so fair."

"Ah, silly flatterer," his mother said, taking the love-lock tied with blue ribbon in her hand. "And is there a lady-love fairer than thy mother who toys with this, as thou sittest at her feet? Is there no true woman, as well as fair, who will fill the place in my heart as thy wife which our sainted Martha left empty? Yes, as thy wife, Edward, give me an elder daughter to love."

"There is no one that has touched my heart

as yet, sweet mother. I see many fair faces, and hear soft voices; but I am not favoured by the maidens; they think me solemn and sombre, and like better those men who can play on a lute, or sing songs, and roll off flattering speeches. Those I cannot—nor would I if I could."

"She will come at last, please God, the right lady; perhaps a Spanish maiden, with dark eyes and crimson cheeks, like the damask rose. We will wait for her, dear boy. And now, what think you of our taking the barge down the river, and eating our supper on the turf? We can explore the woods at Leigh, and listen to the nightingales. Thy father seemed pleased that we should have the barge, and it will be a rare treat to get out of the city this summer evening. We must start at four of the clock. Will the maidens from Mary le Port Street be in readiness?"

"I will go and summon them," Edward Colston said, "for I bid them for six o'clock;" and then he went on, "Mother, do you hold much converse with Damaris Standfast?"

"Aye; do I not? Whenever I can get the chance. Dear Damaris! she has had her sorrows but they have but refined and purified her."

"What sorrows?" Edward Colston asked.

"A brave boy who loved her, fell with young Pugsley, fighting hand to hand hard by St. Michael's Hill. He was a kinsman of the Pugsleys, and one of the bravest of the brave. Damaris still visits weekly the young widow of the elder Pugsley, and she can never mention that name, though it is twelve years agone, without a sigh."

"Did she love him so well?" Edward Colston asked.

"He was near distracted with love for her," was the reply; "and love begetteth love, Edward."

"Is it always so?" the young man replied. "I think Damaris Standfast is a lovely and beautiful woman. How old is she, mother?"

"She was nearly ten years old when you were lying in the cradle. She is thirty and over. There are many who can scarce credit it. We mothers keep good registers of age; measuring by our own children, we are rarely at fault. The dates are e'en graven in my memory, especially thine, dear son."

Edward Colston took his mother's hand as she drew her needle through her work, and kissed it.

"Sweet mother, if thou wilt find me a woman equal to thyself, why, then, I will love her till death."

"Silly boy! There are many fairer and wiser for thy choice; but, Edward, none who can love thee more enduringly. Now I must go down below, and see that the pasty preparing as a cold viand for our expedition, does not catch the fire. Ah! who comes here?" For the child Will returned, throwing open the door to admit a young gentleman, richly attired in the extreme fashion of the dress of the Cavaliers, which now contrasted so strongly with the Puritan costume, especially in Bristol, where the Mayor and Corporation had made themselves conspicuous of late in their devotion to the Lord Protector, when he commanded them to strengthen the city against a suspected rising in favour of "the man Charles Stuart." There seems to have been amongst the city magnates a good deal of the Vicar of Bray's policy, and at the time of which we now speak, there was a general unanimity in the Council-chamber of adherence to the power that had asserted itself before the whole nation as supreme, on the seventh of June, scarcely a fortnight before. William Colston, sturdy

Royalist as he was, and suffering from his allegiance, wore the sober dress of an elderly gentleman: a full-bottomed wig, long gown, with rich sleeves hanging from the elbow, and decorated sparingly with bows of ribbon, with little puffs on the shoulder. His collar was plain and pointed, and the tight sleeves beneath the open ones were relieved by a wide cuff of the same material as the collar. It was a dress distinct indeed from that of Puritan and Quaker, but very far below the splendour of costume which now broke in upon Mistress Colston's boudoir.

"Master Hyacinth Sacheverell, at your service," the young man said. "Master Colston, to whom I bare letters of commendation, bid me seek you, madam. He is just now in deep converse with a grave divine, and methinks I was in the way of their learned discourse. I affect not learning."

"I bid you welcome, sir," Mistress Colston said, with a certain stately dignity which seemed to strike her visitor, for his tone was less self-asserting as he made another low bow, and, turning to Edward Colston, said,

"Master Edward Colston, methinks?"

The contrast between the two young men

was marked indeed. Both about the same age, and both merchants' sons, and coming of a stock loyal to the king and the church. But Master Hyacinth Sacheverell was in manner and bearing a "gay cavalier." His love-lock lay on a collar of the richest lace; his vest was of thick brocade, and his short coat, of velvet. A cape turned back displayed a lining of ruby satin. Heavy ruffles of lace lay on the cuffs of his coat, and his short breeches were tied with ruby ribbons. The hat, which he held in his hand, was heavy with white plumes, and the kilt of his rapier glistened with pure brilliants set in chased silver.

Edward Colston's attire was sober indeed when compared with the new-comer's, and his always stiff sedate manner seemed even more sedate and stiff than usual.

"I come," Hyacinth Sacheverell said, "from my father, a merchant in the more northern part of England. He has had communication with Master Colston concerning me. He would fain make a merchant of me, and thinks that Bristol is the school wherein I am to learn my trade. But I would not trouble you, fair lady, with business. Forsooth, an' you hate the name as much as I do, you will not care to hear more of it now."

"All things in their proper place," was Mistress Colston's reply. "We are making holiday to-day, and purpose taking the barge down the river. We shall find your company pleasant, if you will join us."

"Indeed will I. I rode from Macclesfield in the heat yesterday, and have slept late. The river will be a pleasant change, forsooth."

"Then I will commend you to my son for entertainment while I make some arrangements which are needful for our repast. Forget not to summon Damaris and Margery in good time, Edward," Mistress Colston said as she left the room.

"Your mother is still fair and stately," Hyacinth said, as he threw himself on one of the low benches by the window, stretching out his legs and resting his head on his hand in an easy, graceful position. "And are Damaris and Margery your sisters? I hope they are fair buds, worthy of the full-blown rose which has just quitted us."

"My sister at home is a child of tender years," was Colston's reply. "The elder, Nan, lives with an aunt. The gentlewomen mentioned by my mother are neighbours and friends."

"Ah, ha! perhaps something nearer and dearer. Spare me one, prythee. You can't take two to your share; that is too covetous."

Edward Colston's face flushed with colour like a girl's who shrinks from the jester's rude banter, and Hyacinth laughed merrily.

"Nay, now, man, can'st not take a joke? I pray you are not all Puritans and Quakers here, or I shall be off whence I came, for all my father can say. To tell truth, I think he fancies that the sober-going folks in your ancient city will be as wholesome drugs to me. I am to be sent to Spain by your father, if I suit him. You are to go also, methinks."

"It is not brought to any point of settlement yet," was the reply. "I have only lately returned to Bristol, after years of absence."

"Well, if we go together we had as well be friends. We won't quarrel over the two fair neighbours—for I warrant they are fair. Have you been peaceable in this city of late?" Hyacinth contrived to turn the subject into another channel, as he saw Edward Colston's brow grew increasingly dark.

"I'd rather like to see a riot, and I'm all agog to have a fling at the Quakers. Poor fools! they seem to have planted their folly here with a vengeance. Mine host of the White Lion has a long tongue, and told me of the sticking of that obstinate pig Naylor. I would I had been here to see."

"You might have had the sight and welcome, for me," said Edward Colston. "Much as I hate the fanatics, I detest cruelty. It were wiser to teach them better, than maim and bruise them for their ignorance."

The young men's conversation was now interrupted by the entrance of Edward's father, who, with apologies for leaving his guest so long, begged him to consider the house his home for the time being, and added, "We will discuss this letter I hold in my hand from your worshipful father more fully anon. The young folks here are to make holiday to-day in the woods below Leigh. So we will defer business till a future day. Edward, conduct Master Hyacinth Sacheverell to a guest chamber, and make him welcome."

A HUNTED HARE.

VERY charming did Margery Standfast look in her white sarcenet and velvet bodice, with her lace-trimmed apron, and cherry-coloured ribbons. When she had completed her attire, she ran lightly downstairs, and, crossing a narrow strip of paved court, tapped at a door, which was opened immediately by a woman with a serene, sweet face, and meek, gentle voice.

"I am come to be looked at, Cicely," Margery exclaimed; "prythee, see that my bodice closes properly at the back, and give my skirts a smoothing hand; and—well—just tell me if I look in proper guise for a holiday. I have let my hair fall adown my shoulders to-day; it seems a pity to tuck it up. Now, Cicely, don't look so grave, and as if I were a sinner. Doth not Paul the apostle say the hair is the woman's glory? I verily believe you would like to see me in a thick white cap, and an ugly brown gown. Cicely, it would make me no whit better at heart.

"Dear child," said Cicely, looking at Margery with eyes of loving admiration, mingled with a wistful sadness, "far be it from me to preach doctrine like that, but when the heart is filled with holy love and fear, there is no room for undue care for gauds and finery. Mistake me not, the outward man or woman is of less moment than we are prone to think."

"Thy children are keeping Damaris hard at their tasks; they are such demure little creatures, I would fain see them restive; is it the iron rule of their father which has made them look on laughter as a sin?"

Cicely Purdy took no heed of this remark of Margery's, but said with a sigh, "These are sad and evil times, dear heart. I have a poor girl in my upper chamber whose case makes my heart sore. She came in like a hunted hare, yester even, and I cannot turn her forth."

"Who is she? Let me see her."

"Better not, methinks; it might cause trouble. She is the child of poor Sarah Goldsmith, who has languished in a dark and fetid dungeon for near two years, and——"

"What, the mad Quaker woman, who walked through the streets in a long hairy coat, one market day! Dreadful and loathsome creature;

I remember, I caught sight of her, and was nearly sick. It is worse for a woman to do such bold things than for a man like Naylor, though my father says he was cruelly used, and that by ignorance; for that the way the Quakers are used is like to make them madder than before. I dare say now this girl in thy chamber is mad?"

"No," said Cicely Purdy, "she is calm and quiet; but she is nearly famishing; she feels the Spirit of the Lord is within her to guide her right. May it prove so."

"Does Will Purdy know of her being beneath thy roof?"

"Yes, verily, Margery; a wife conceals nothing from her husband, or she forgets her duty strangely. That is a lesson you must learn, dear child."

"Find me the husband first, Cicely, then I'll con the task. Husband, indeed! It is not in our way to find husbands. A stiff, solemn young man has set foot in our house, 'tis true, this day, but he looks as if he could care for nought but himself. Damaris is pleased to say she affects him, and that you will mind taking her to visit him a babe in the cradle."

"What, is it Master Edward Colston? Ah,

verily, I do mind it, and how I laid thee near the babe, and Mistress Colston said——"

"What did she say?" as Cicely paused.

"That you and her boy were a sweet pair, and Damaris, with her quick tongue in those days, said, 'Nay, not a pair, for one is so much bigger and older than t'other.'"

"To think of it!" said Margery. "I'd pity his pair, with his old, old face and manners like a minister. I like something livelier, forsooth. Here come thy children, Cicely, from their tasks. What a troop!"

The mother's face glowed with maternal pride as her rosy-cheeked sons and daughters, two of each, came in from their lessons with Damaris. It was wonderful that such roses should bloom in a court at the back of Mary le Port Street, under the shadow of the large storehouses. But early hours and plain food, with a general regularity of routine, did much towards maintaining the health of Cicely Purdy's household. And her sweet temper was inherited by her children. What snarling and contradiction there was came from Will Purdy, who, like many another man who has been wild in youth, had become strict and even fanatical in his religious observances and demeanour. His appearance was the signal for Margery to take flight, and as Will Purdy came from a door in one direction, Margery escaped in the other, calling out, in her bird-like treble,

"I wish you good-day, Master Purdy."

Will Purdy groaned, and turned up his eyes as he turned into his own house, where, in an inner room, the mid-day meal was prepared; wooden bowls of furmity with a little spice for the children, and a trencher of savoury beef for the father and mother. There was nothing stronger than water drunk at the table, and the repast had no variety except the crisp rolls of sugared bread, which were thought a great dainty by the little Purdys. A long grace, or rather exordium, which was meant to be thanksgiving, but sounded very like the invocation of some offended and angry power, far out of sight and reach, preceded the meal, and then Cicely said:

"I think, dear heart, I would fain see how it fares with poor Grace, and take her a roll and a cup of water."

"It is more seemly to eat thy own meal first, Cicely," said Will Purdy. "How long shall this poor creature abide under our roof?"

"I cannot tell, dear Will. I would fain keep her from the rude and rough folk, whose licence is unbridled, and whose wrath is poured forth—they know not why—on the harmless Quakers."

"Harmless, forsooth! But I am not so sure thereof. They have made strife in the city, and of some it may be said that they grin like dogs, and go hither and thither."

"Methinks," said his wife, gently, "that there are some who deem us, who meet together to praise the Lord under men who are chosen for gifts of grace in the churches in place of those who worshipped and followed idols, no less fanatical and mad than the followers of George Fox. I can look back to the little secret meetings in Mistress Kelly's, now Mistress Hassard's, house, and the riot and strife they occasioned once," she said, going round to the bench where Will Purdy sat. "And I recall, Will, how a strong arm saved me from harm."

"The Lord was thy deliverer, sweetheart. To Him be the praise," said Will Purdy, with a sanctimonious drawl and uplifting of the eyes, which he deemed proper for the occasion. "The Corporation have decreed a solemn fast for the first day of July. Master Howe will minister to us from nine of the clock in the morning to nine in the evening. Joan and Dick are old enow to be with us throughout. Come hither, Joan; thou wilt like to worship as a grown woman, and lie in abasement before God?"

Joan's large eyes opened wide in wonder, and she glanced at her mother for some sign to guide her in her reply. But Dick spoke out with alarming boldness.

"Nay, father, an it please you, I love not the long worship. I sleep instead of praying, and then Joan diggeth a pin into my calf and I dare not call out, and—"

"Hush, Dick, hush!" said his mother, terrified at the boy's rashness, and fearing her husband's anger. "See, when thy father has given thanks, thou shalt help me to clear the board, and Joan shall take the two little ones forth to breathe the air on the quay; it is too hot this summer day in the city."

"I would fain go with Joan," said Dick, "or in her place."

"Nay, nay; thou art not to be trusted with Elisha and little Jemima. Joan is steady. But hush now."

Will Purdy stood up to conclude the meal with a similar religious exercise as that with which he had begun, and then sternly calling Dick to him, took down a cane from a shelf and administered to the boy some sharp cuts across the shoulders, saying:

"It is the Lord's will that I should show my son that to speak lightly of an exercise of faith is hateful in His eyes."

The boy winced a little under the lash, but he did not cry out. The stern Puritans early taught their children to endure hardness, and Dick, though with a swelling heart, and one furtive glance at his mother's flushed cheeks, did not utter a sound, but taking up the trencher and one of the bowls, he ran off to the kitchen and set himself to the business in hand.

When Joan had departed with the two younger children, Dick and his mother were left alone at their household occupation; and Cicely laid her hand on the boy's head, with soft caressing touch.

"Good boy!" she said tenderly; "brave boy! It behoves a father never to spare the rod—it is so ordained by God."

Dick looked up at her, his heart still smarting

under a sense of injustice as his back did with the twinges that the cane had given him, and said:

"Mother, is it like to do harm when the rod is used for nought but speaking the truth? And those poor creatures who are punished for a walk on Sunday are in the same case. Why does God suffer such wrongs?"

"Dear boy, thou art too young to speak of these matters; the judgment of children must be submitted to that of elders. For some years after my marriage with thy father, Dick, the Lord refused to give me the blessing of a son. At last, as Samuel was sent to Hannah in answer to her prayer, thou wert sent to me. See to it, Richard, that my heart may sing for joy concerning thee, nor give me pain by forsaking the ways of peace."

When his mother spoke to him with her grave sweet voice, Richard felt as if for her sake he would endure fasts and buffetings, and forego all the pleasures in which boys of ten years old delight.

But when his father rated him for innocent mirth, and made the day of Rest a day of penance, forbidding a smile or a light word, forcing even a baby like little Jemima to bow to his will, then the boy's whole nature rose up in rebellious desire to burst his bonds and be free. His lessons with Damaris were one of his few pleasures, but of these he was afraid to speak.

The beautiful and gracious woman was no favourite of Will Purdy's. He did not forget that she could recall him in his gay reckless days, and, as he expressed it, before the Hand of the Lord had turned him from the ways of sin to the paths of holiness.

Will Purdy had sown his wild oats, and now he wished to forget that he had ever been the young apprentice who was the ringleader of many riots, and danced and sang—yes, and drank also, on the Lord's Day. A change for the better who shall doubt? but William Purdy like many, ah, how many in our own day, missed the spirit of His Master, and would fain drive others to believe that He delighted in the crushing out of all natural affection and joys. It was the old ascetic spirit taking a new form.

The Puritan carried into the world the austerities and self-annihilation which the monks hid in the cloister. And the narrow plank on which Will Purdy marched trying to drive everyone before him on it as the only way of safety, is that on which in all ages of the Church, he who utterly lacks sympathy has made many an earnest soul to stumble.

As Richard and his mother were thus talking together, another visitor appeared.

Damaris Standfast had also donned her holiday garments, of a more sober hue than her young sister's, but of rich dark colours admirably fitted to set off her beauty. Her dark hair was combed back and fell on her shoulders, beneath a velvet hood, pointed on the forehead, her full dark prune gown was open in front and displayed a petticoat of rich amber. The sleeves of her gown were short and turned back with a cuff, and she wore long loosely-fitting gloves on her beautiful arms.

"Ah! Dick," she said, "I am right glad to see you helping your mother;" and going up to Cicely, Damaris kissed her affectionately.

"We are going to make holiday with Mistress Colston and her children to-day, dear Cicely. I came to ask if you would sit a short space with poor mother. She is very sad to-day, and Hannah is in one of her crabbed moods. She is getting past her work, and we must get a young girl to relieve her. The poor mother asks for the same thing a hundred times, and she must needs have her rich gowns out, and be decked in her finery. Oh, Cicely, my heart is sore for her. I would fain move my father to let her be taken to a room in a farm or old Manor for the summer months; but he says it would be no better there than here."

"I will go, and gladly, to the poor mistress when I have set things in order here; but, Damaris, I have a hunted hare in an upper chamber, the child of that unhappy woman, Sarah Goldsmith. She was speaking in a room in Corn Street yestereven, as she said the spirit moved her, and the rough folk hunted her and a few others into the street, belabouring them with sticks and stones, which have left their marks on the poor tender girl's shoulders and arms. Alas! that there should be such hard hearts. I found her crouched under one of the large vats in the court when I came in from worship, and I got her upstairs, and they have lost the scent."

Damaris' dark eyes flashed.

"The cravens, the cowards, to attack a feeble girl! I have no great kindness for the Quakers, but, oh, I loathe persecution. Let me see her, Cicely. I have yet a few minutes."

"I am taking her up some broth," Cicely

said, "and a roll. Here, Dick, hand me the small wooden bowl and the platter."

Then Cicely began to mount the narrow, uneven staircase, which was winding and steep. Will Purdy's house was built at the back of Thomas Standfast's, on one side of the broad courtyard. Light and air were, as I have said, scarce in the lower part of the dwelling; but here, in the top story, there was a view of the river, and the shipping, and the green hills beyond, while the tower of St. Mary Redcliffe showed clear against the summer sky.

Seated on a stool by the window was a young girl, with eager, wistful eyes, and a pinched thin face. Her hair was closely cut, and she wore a plain cap with a frill. Her stuff gown was much torn and spotted, and the muslin kerchief which Cicely had lent her—her own being torn and covered with mud—was the only fresh thing about her.

"Dear child," Cicely said, "I have brought you some food. See, now; and here is a kind gentlewoman whose heart aches for thy wrongs."

The poor girl turned a sad, half-bewildered gaze on Damaris, and said:

"Didst thou ever hear George Fox?"

"No," Damaris said, "dear child; and I

would you had not heard him either. He works much mischief."

"Ah!" said the girl, throwing her arms above her head in an excited manner, "thou knowest not what thou sayest. The spirit—the free spirit of light and liberty—hath not touched thy heart. Thou standest there in all that gay apparel, and yet art in darkness, and shouldst wear sackcloth."

Damaris' beautiful eyes were full of compassion, and she said gently:

"I grieve that you should have had such rough handling; stay, now, in this shelter, afforded by my good friend Cicely Purdy, and to-morrow I will see you again, and we will devise some means for your safety."

"And, prythee, eat what I have brought thee," Cicely said; "it will give thee some strength."

The girl shook her head.

"I feel choked when I eat, and my mother is in a dungeon, starving and forlorn. Ah, that the Omnipotent should suffer the rod of the ungodly to triumph!"

Damaris looked round, and seeing the mattress and rug in the corner, she said:

"Eat this broth, and then lie down to sleep.

See, I will feed you," she said, "poor child, my heart is drawn to you in love and pity;" and, sitting down on the bench by the side of the poor forlorn wanderer, she put her arm round her, and as Cicely held the bowl, she fed her with a small spoonful at a time.

The girl grew quieter, and then Damaris led her to the bed and laid her down, saying gently, "Sleep, now, and I will return ere long, and talk with you of the future."

"I thought," the girl sighed, "I thought the grand women of the world, like thee, despised us, hated us, and spurned us, and thou—thou seemest to be full of love."

"Ah, yes!" said Cicely, "that is true. My dear mistress and friend, Damaris Standfast, liveth for others, and forgets herself in loving deeds."

"Nay, nay, not so," the girl exclaimed, "or she would forsake those gauds which savour of the world. Nay, nay, tempt me not to say that she is right, nay, nay."

"She is worn out with excitement and fatigue, Cicely, and I will come in this evening if we return in time. Dear Cicely, I wish you were coming to the woods with us."

"I have much work at home to get through,

and I have no time for mere play," Cicely said gravely. "I would fain see Master Edward Colston. I heard what a brave boy he was when he was here ten years agone."

"Ah, yes, that time is a blank to me," Damaris said. "Cicely, I marvel often when I think of my loss, that I can be gay again. Methinks I have seen times of trouble that might well make me a grave or sad woman. Instead of that, there is in me some secret spring of joy that bubbles up when I see the trees and the sky, and hear the dear birds sing."

"Ah, dear heart," Cicely said, " may thy love yet crown some good man's life with blessings. She is quiet now, we will leave her, and I must to my household cares, and then betake to the poor mistress's chamber.

Cicely and Damaris then went down the narrow stairs together; and Dick announced that he had seen two grand gentlemen entering Master Standfast's house, and that one was clothed in velvet and feathers, and he heard his father say he was even as a limb of the evil one.

ON THE RIVER.

THE water traffic of the seventeenth century was scarcely yet declining. The barges of the nobility were, like the carriages of the present day, a token of the wealth and prosperity of their owners. The Thames presented a lively scene as the barges, with gay trappings and pennons flying, skimmed its broad surface, and the sound of music was often borne upon the summer breeze as the barges glided past the gardens sloping from the Strand to the water's edge, as a gay bevy of ladies and gentlemen returned from an expedition to Gravesend or Richmond Park, where on summer evenings the nightingales sang their sweet, plaintive song.

And, though in a less degree, the sombre waters of the Avon were often alive with the craft of the merchants and principal citizens of Old Bristol, the Mayor and Aldermen had their state barges, and private barges also. William Colston's was richly appointed, and the seats luxurious with soft cushions. It was not often now that he used his barge for a pleasure trip; but to-day he had yielded to his wife's entreaties, and about four o'clock was handing his guests down the steps by the bridge, and taking care that the boat was well trimmed. Several servants were in attendance with the dainty fare Mistress Colston had provided, and Edward's younger brothers and little Mall were included in the company.

Master Hyacinth Sacheverell might have preferred the children's room to their company; but, leaning back in easy fashion on one of the soft cushioned benches, he was well content to watch the objects of interest as they passed, and roll out a succession of flattering speeches to his fair neighbours, Damaris and Margery Standfast.

As the giant St. Vincent's Rock rose to the right, and the cathedral, followed by the slopes of Leigh Down and Ashton, opened to the left, Master Hyacinth allowed himself to show some sign of admiration. He raised himself on his elbow, and declared that in all the wild fastnesses of the Peak, in his native county, there was nothing so mighty grand as these huge walls of rock.

"Indeed," he said, "I came to Bristol expect-

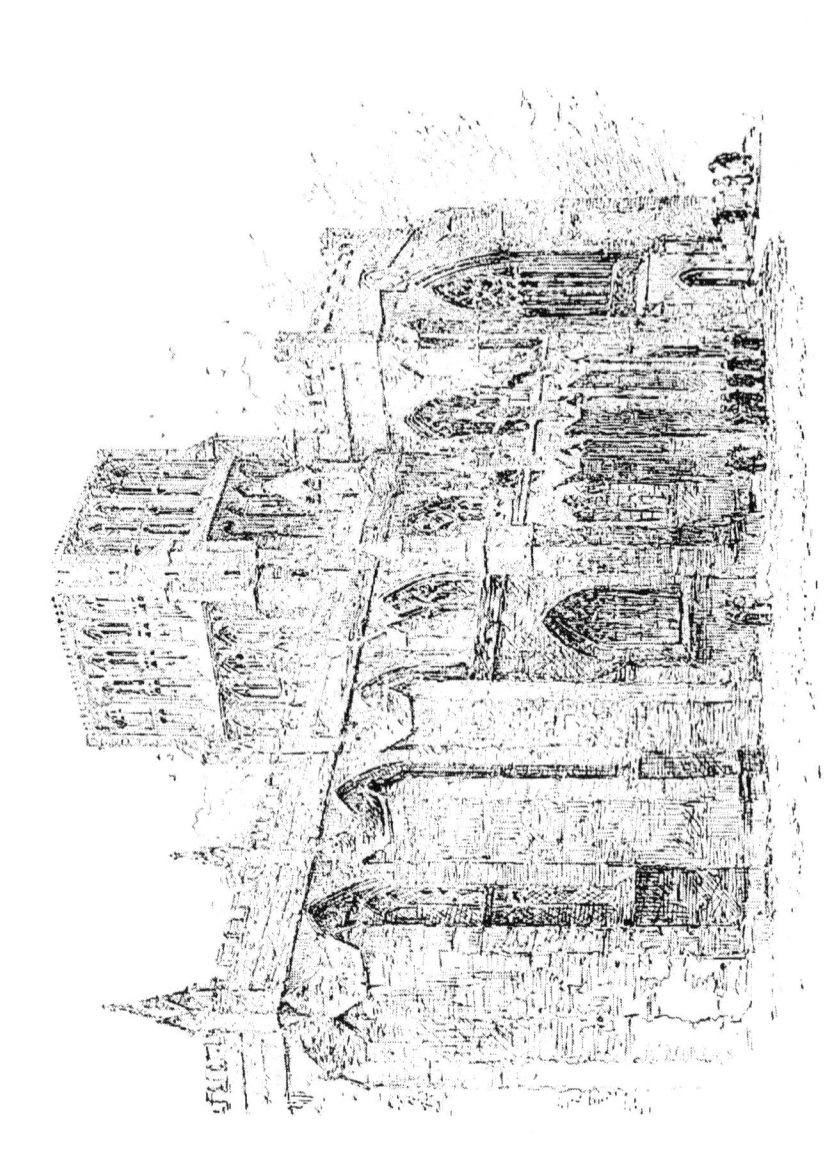

THE CATHEDRAL.

ing to find a prison, and I find a Paradise, with fair ladies beyond compare. Master Colston, you gave my father no hint of this."

"Your father knows well the rocks are very fine. He was here before you were born, and I mind that I walked with him by the river side. I was a young man then," and William Colston sighed.

"Thou art not old now, dear heart," said his wife; "and the days are coming when I shall see thee young again."

William Colston shook his head.

"I leave youth to thee, sweetheart, and to our little Mall. See, Master Hyacinth, yonder road leads up to Abbot Leigh, across Rownham Ferry, where his Majesty, our present gracious King Charles the Second, was so nobly aided in his flight by Mistress Norton."

The young man turned his head lazily in the direction pointed out, and addressing Margery, said:

"You can scarce recall that time, fair Mistress Margery?"

"Nay, that I can, and Damaris will have it that I can mind the day when the blessed King Charles slept under Master Colston's roof. She says she knelt and kissed his hand, and led me forward to do the same, and I was stubborn and said I would not kneel. Damaris! for all you say, you might be a mute—Damaris!"

Damaris thus appealed to, roused herself from her dream, and said,

"What need for me to talk, Margery, when thy tongue runs so glibly?"

"Forsooth, you and Master Edward Colston have sworn a solemn league and covenant that you would be silent. Methinks," exclaimed Master Hyacinth, "that you might enliven us with a word."

"So many words spoken by you, Master Hyacinth, leave but little room for others."

Hyacinth laughed, and calling little Mall to him, he fed her with comfits from a silver box he wore in his doublet.

The barge went slowly down the river, and then tacking at Pylle, the party were put on land just as the first lofty slopes, covered with trees in all their emerald freshness, climbed towards the summit of the Leigh Downs. In one of the glades shaded by the feathery birches, with their silver boles catching the sunshine here and there, the repast was spread.

The young Colstons delighted to assist in the preparations for the *al fresco* entertainment, while the elders wandered in the glades and through the winding paths, and listened to the glad chorus of the birds in the branches above them. Here and there fragments of limestone cropped up and were inviting as seats.

Edward Colston and Damaris had strolled up the valley by a path which turned abruptly to the right, and Damaris sat down on a ledge of rock. Her companion did not throw himself into a graceful attitude at her feet, as Master Hyacinth would have done, but stood erect, leaning against the trunk of a tree.

"Do you often visit this spot, Mistress Damaris?" Edward Colston asked, by way of breaking the silence.

"Not often," Damaris replied; "it is a long distance from the city, and my father has no barge; he hires a craft when he takes the water. But," she continued, with an earnestness which was seen in the tight clasp of her hands as they rested on her lap, "but, oh! it is verily a heart-joy to be here! The air is so sweet and fresh—the quiet only broken by the singing of the birds. It is hard to believe, Master Colston, that the toiling city, with all the sorrow and sin enclosed within its gates, is so near."

"Yes, indeed, it is so," Edward Colston replied. "These are great perplexities for us when we think of the sin and sorrow of which you spake; and there is nothing to be done, I fear me."

"Nothing to be done!" Damaris said, repeating his words. "Ah! verily I will not hold that doctrine. I have a friend"—she paused for a moment, and then went on—"I have a friend who has tried for years how to discover what she can do, and though but a weak woman, she has found the clue. She is Dame Pugsley, whose dear lord fell in the fight at Prior's Hill, when Fairfax's army made such dire havoc on the Montpellier heights and those people of Bristol lost the city and forts; aye, and lost too many a brave and noble heart with it. A healing stream, as you may know, Master Colston, springs up just by the spot, and here Dame Pugsley comes to mourn her lost love; but to mourn wisely, not sorrowing as with no hope. She tends the sick, she instructs the ignorant, she teaches the children. 'For,' saith she, 'therein lies the strength of our future, that the English people should be well taught, for how many err from sheer ignorance?'"

Edward Colston's eyes glistened with sympathy as Damaris spoke these words.

"Aye," he said, "the lady's life of whom you speak is worth living; and you are like-minded with her, Mistress Damaris."

"Mine is but a small work," Damaris said; "but it lies near me, and so if I do it, it may haply bring a blessing or leave one. I do but put the children of my father's servants in his warehouses and storehouses through some tasks suited to their age. I would fain do more, but the time is not yet come. It seemeth to me, Master Colston, that we who live in these times must needs acknowledge with shame, that we have not followed as benefactors of the poor, those who went before us, even though they belonged to the Church filled with errors, growing on the stately tree as fungi on yon witch elm, deforming its beauty and sapping its strength. I have lived thirty full years, and what have I not seen of the perils of ignorance? Think you, if these poor folk of our realm were instructed as children, instead of being treated as we treat beasts of burden to work for us, and live with no thought of better and higher aims, no recreation for mind or body—think you they would have joined in the outcry against king and Church, and, as in our old city of Bristol, clamoured for the life of the blessed king one day, and repented themselves in the next. They know not, poor souls, wherefore they do thus."

Edward Colston listened to Damaris with wrapt attention. She looked beautiful in her earnestness, and her whole face was aglow as she spoke.

"I am old for my years," she went on, "though these years are thirty; and I remember you in your cradle."

"Methinks that is a dream," Edward Colston said with a smile. "Methinks the order is reversed, and I am the senior."

"Nay, will you see a token of it?" and Damaris drew from her large pocket, worn suspended from her girdle, a small silver box, and unscrewing the lid, she said:

"See the letters within :—'W.C. to D.S., 1636.' Your good father gave me this token of his favour on the day after your baptism feast in Small Street. I have borne it about with me ever since."

Edward Colston took the box from Damaris and said:

"Nay, I cannot gainsay so sure a token. And your sister, had she a like offering?

"She would fain have possessed herself of this bauble. I mind well how she stretched out her hand for it. Poor Margery! But—but they are calling us to go down to the supper," and Damaris rose.

"Come, Mistress Damaris," shouted one of Edward's young brothers; "they are all impatient to fall to, and nowhere can be found you or Mistress Margery. She and the grand young gentleman have, like you, hidden themselves."

"They are making a love story, doubtless," said the younger of the boys; "and perchance you are following their example."

"Peace, you idle chatterer!" said Edward Colston, angrily; "methinks your manners need mending."

"But where is Margery?" Damaris said, rather anxiously. "She has not passed up this way, and it is not safe to penetrate too far within the woods. There are often persons with evil intent lurking on the Leigh Downs. It is ill-chosen of Margery to stray so far and with a stranger."

She was descending the rugged path now, looking from right to left, and pausing every few steps to listen, when a sound in an old gnarled oak arrested her. It was a low silvery laugh above her head.

"It sounds like a magpie," said Edward Colston. "They——"

"Thank you, Master Colston, for so pretty a compliment," said a voice above him.

"It is Margery playing us a trick," Damaris exclaimed. "How could she get up that tree?"

"How did his gracious Majesty King Charles scale an oak?" said another voice. "Methinks I am minded to stay here all night, even if I must feed on black bread and small ale."

And then, as those at the foot of the tree looked up, the gay colours of Master Hyacinth Sacheverell's attire caught the slanting sunbeams which were now sending golden shafts of glory through the branches of the trees, and showed like the plumage of a macaw, while a silvery streak showed where Margery's white silk glistened like the wings of a dove.

Damaris spoke gravely as she said—"The supper is awaiting us; get down from your high perch, Margery."

"Rather come up and join us," said Master Sacheverell; "it is a comfortable seat. Master Colston will help you to ascend."

But Damaris only repeated, "Come down,

Margery;" while Edward Colston put one foot on one of the rough knots of the trunk, as if to help Margery to descend.

Instantly, with a light spring, Margery had reached a lower branch, and in another moment was standing by her sister's side, while her *preux chevalier* came down more cautiously, having respect to the lace on his cuffs, and not wishing to leave green marks from the tree upon his crimson velvet coat.

"That was a perilous leap, Mistress Margery," said Edward Colston; "and methinks those who had placed you in danger by climbing should have taken care that you were not hurt in the venture."

"I am not hurt; why should you say so?" Margery exclaimed, putting her hand within Damaris's arm. "Nay, sister mine, do not look so grave. It is rare indeed for me to have a holiday; let me make the most of it. Bid her not to scold me, Master Edward Colston, though you look as if you would like to scold me yourself."

"Then I look what I do not feel," was the reply, as they reached the greensward, where the supper was spread.

The stars were coming out in the dark blue sky before the party took the barge homewards.

Little Mall slept in her mother's arms; the boys, tired with their frolics in the wood, subsided into quiet.

The gentle ripple of the water against the prow made a low accompaniment to the song of the nightingales, heard from the slopes on both sides of the river.

The twilight lent enchantment to the view, and the towers of the churches of St. Stephen and St. Werburgh, and masses of gabled roofs stood out against the sky as the barge neared the quay. Here and there a torch flickered, and boys were seen carrying them before some party of citizens who had been out on pleasure.

Voices, too, were heard from the open windows of one of the houses near the quay, raised in the loud strains of some hymn of praise, or denouncing of God's wrath on the impenitent sinner.

ST. STEPHEN'S.

The Puritans held meetings now in many houses, and they were seldom disturbed; while the Quakers were hunted out, and beaten and ill-treated—sometimes "done to death"—and no one interfered. But to-night, outwardly, all was calm in the city, and in the heart of one at least of that party on board the barge, great thoughts were stirring.

The future stretched out dimly before him. A foreign country was to be his home. The wide machinery whereby his father's trade made money, and gathered up riches, was to be entrusted to him. There was breaking in upon the young man's soul even then the light which should show him that silver and gold could only be safely used when consecrated to the service of others for Christ's sake. His thoughts might not take any definite shape or plan; but a soft, musical voice seemed to sound again and again in his ear—

"Nothing to be done! Aye, verily, I will not hold that doctrine."

Something might be done; and though, as she said, her work was small, was she not faithfully fulfilling it?

Edward Colston ventured to draw a little nearer to Damaris, and said:

"Will you be pleased to take me to see your friend Dame Pugsley?"

His voice startled her. She had been lost in her meditations again, and had left her bright young sister to take what part was necessary in the conversation.

"Methinks I should like to visit such a gentle-woman," he added, "and with you."

"I will gladly do so; and she will teach you that something is to be done, *must* be done for those who are perishing for lack of care. It will be done," she added, "and that before many years are gone."

It was almost as if Damaris were gifted with the prescience of what was to come to her native city from the strong hand which was placed in hers as they sat together.

"Let us ratify our old friendship, Mistress Damaris," Edward Colston said. "You knew me in my cradle, you say, though methinks still it is a dream. I would fain have you as a wise counsellor and friend, an so it please you."

"It pleases me well," she answered, in a low, firm tone; "and you shall never count on my friendship in vain."

There was always something grave and almost solemn in Edward Colston's manner;

and, as he said, he was not one who could bandy light words, or coin flattering speeches. But Damaris had lived through too many scenes of trouble and sorrow for herself and others, to have any taste for the frivolity which the Royalists seemed to assume as their right, and delighted to flaunt as their colours before the eyes of the stern and rigid Puritans. There was a great deal of unreality and affectation on both sides, and many a gaily-dressed cavalier bore a sad heart beneath his rich doublet, and many a stiff Puritan or Roundhead was weary of his bondage, and chafed under the very fetters he had himself forged.

"I may visit you often, Mistress Damaris? You will give me leave to do so? Our families have long been united in the cause of Church and King."

"You will be welcome to my father's house," Damaris said, with a touch of stately dignity in her voice and manner, as she drew her hooded mantle closely around her, and bid Margery do the same; for the evening air was chill, and the dew falling after the heat of the long summer day.

ROYAL ROBES.

Poor Mistress Standfast was but a wreck of her former self. She had been one of the sufferers from the Plague in its last visitation, and though she was one of the rare instances of recovery, she was shattered in body and mind henceforth.

The ruling passion was strong in Mistress Standfast, and the one delight of her dull monotonous days was to have all her gay attire spread before her, and get her waiting-woman Hannah, or Cicely Purdy, to dress her in some of her fine garments.

The care and management of the sick was but little understood in those days, and invalids like Mistress Standfast were left very much to themselves.

No attempts were made to change the scene or vary the monotony of the sick-room.

Twice a day Thomas Standfast visited his wife, and would stroke her hand and kiss her forehead and say, " Poor thing ! " The doctor had no suggestions to make beyond letting a little blood from the arm at intervals. Margery flitted into the room once a day, but disliked to stay there, and even Damaris only spent a certain time with her step-mother from a sense of duty.

Cicely Purdy had the most soothing influence over the poor forsaken invalid, and as Hannah became more and more infirm, her services were in great request.

On the day of the expedition on the river, Mistress Standfast had been unusually restless and hard to please. The sight of her young daughter dressed in her holiday garments had awoke a sort of longing for health and liberty to go hither and thither. And when Cicely went to her after her household duties were over she found her crying piteously.

Hannah was snoring heavily in a settle by the wood fire, which even on this hot June day was not unwelcome in the large room with its vaulted ceiling, which only commanded a view of the quadrangle, on one side of which Will Purdy's dwelling, as I have described it, stood.

Cicely Purdy generally contrived to soothe and cheer her poor mistress; and, treating her like a child, she talked to her as to one of her own little ones.

It was plain that old Hannah must soon be relieved of her duties. She was past work, and some one must be found to fill her place.

This afternoon it struck Cicely that the poor girl who had taken refuge with her, Grace Goldsmith, the wild Quaker-woman's child, might be of use, and that she would be secure from discovery if in Thomas Standfast's house.

"Cicely, Cicely!" Mistress Standfast called out. "Get out the brocade taffeta, and the train edged with gold, and that lace veil which was my great-grandmother's, and help me to dress."

"The gown will be too heavy for you, dear mistress," Cicely said. "You look pale and weary."

"I had the Plague, Cicely, and it made me ill; but I shall be quite well soon. I must needs get ready for court, for the king always loves to have the FitzHardinges about him. Quick, Cicely! Why could I not go to the woods with Margery? It is cruel to keep me here—cruel—cruel!"

"Dear mistress," Cicely said, unlocking the bureau, "it would be too much fatigue for you to dress grandly, and go a-pleasuring; but you shall look at the beautiful taffeta and the rich train, an it please you. But we must all look forward to a royal robe, which the King will bestow on us when we enter His court above."

"Royal robes! I would I had them now. What colour are they, Cicely?"

"White—pure white—whiter than snow," Cicely said, "but shining like silver. They were bought for us, dear mistress, by the blood of the Lord Jesus."

"Royal robes — royal robes!" Mistress Standfast repeated. "Whiter than Margery's—better than Damaris's, who looks so proud and vain."

"Nay, nay, dear mistress, that is far from being so: dear Damaris thinks but little of herself. I am right glad she should have gone to Leigh with Master Edward Colston."

"His christening feast! Ah! she wanted sorely to be at that. Well, well, she has had her time now, and, Cicely, I must have mine again."

And then, after some minutes more of wandering in past times, Cicely soothed her; and taking out her Bible, began to read in her clear, sweet voice, the description of the heavenly city, which always seemed to arrest the attention of poor Mistress Standfast.

Altogether she was more reasonable this

evening, and her face had a brighter expression on it.

When Cicely closed the Bible, she asked for the children, and Cicely told her of the poor persecuted girl who was now in the house.

"Beaten and ill-treated; poor thing! Worse than I am, then?"

"Ah! yes, my dear mistress; for she is friendless and homeless."

"Let me see her, let me see her."

"Not to-night, for it is near bed-time; and see, Hannah is preparing your posset."

"Cicely, let me see her to-morrow, and I will tell you a secret. I would like to see something fair and beautiful again, not only old Hannah all day—all day. At night I dream I am wearing all my brave clothes at court—for I have been at the court, and kissed the queen's hand. There is no queen now, is there, Cicely?"

"There are those in high places who take the place of queens and kings," Cicely said earnestly. "And now I must bid you a good-night. Hark, I hear them returning."

As she spoke both Damaris and Margery came in. The twilight still lingered out of doors, but within it was dark.

"Mother, would'st like to see Master Edward Colston?' Margery asked; "he is come home, and will be here to-morrow. He has made love to Damaris, and—"

"Margery, hush! I pray you. It hurts me."

"Now, then, wherefore? Did I not see that piece of perfection, Edward Colston, take your hand? and did he not murmur at the door: 'Permit me to hear what you have written of your memories?' My ears are sharp. Well, while I have Master Hyacinth, I want none of your grave, solemn young Colston. Hark, mother! I will tell you of Master Hyacinth Sacheverell's dress."

"Not to-night, not to-night, Margery. Thy poor mother is tired." For a blank look had again swept over Mistress Standfast's face. But she said, "Royal robes—royal robes! Cicely has promised me some, all glistening with silver."

"She is wandering," Margery exclaimed. "It is of no avail trying to tell her anything;" and she left the room. But Damaris knelt down on a stool by her mother's side, and with womanly tenderness kissed the poor thin hands, and said:

"I have spoken to father as to thy removal to the country, mother. Would you like it?"

"The country! The court is where I want to go—and wear, Cicely, royal robes—silver and white robes."

Thomas Standfast now came slowly into the room, and sat down by his wife. She had ever been a care to him, and of but little comfort; but he felt for her in her low, helpless condition the sort of yearning tenderness which all good men feel for the weak and dependent.

"Well, dear heart," he said, "how fares it with thee? I have been waiting at Master Colston's for those young ones, and took a lonely supper, as they had all fled down the river."

"Have they been to the court?"

"There is no court now," Thomas Standfast sighed. "No king and no court. The usurper hath a pretended one, and thinks himself a king."

"A king—a king—ah!"

Mistress Standfast leaned her head forward, and it fell on Thomas Standfast's arm, which was placed round the chair on which his wife sat.

"Dear husband, we will both wear a royal robe—white and pure—and little Margery and Damaris."

"There is something strange in thy mother to-night," Thomas Sandfast said, addressing Damaris. "Call back Cicely Purdy—send for the doctor, see!"

For Mistress Standfast was slipping from the chair, and would have fallen, had not her husband caught her in his arms and supported her. "Royal robes," she murmured; and Cicely, who had now returned, knelt down by her mistress and said:

"The King will give them to thee, dear mistress; only believe." Then Cicely poured forth a prayer from the very depths of her tender, womanly heart, and Mistress Standfast opened her eyes.

"See," she exclaimed, with a smile, "there is the King!" and then as the light of intelligence faded out and the stillness of death fell over the room, old Hannah's wailing cry broke the silence, but Cicely said,

"Weep not; rather pray that the Lord may accept her of His great mercy."

The funeral of Mistress Standfast took place a few days later, and was largely attended. The beautiful office of the Church could not be used, it was strictly proscribed; but the service was conducted by several lay members, who contrived to infuse into it the spirit of the Church which was now under the ban of Puritan fanaticism. The vault in St. Mary le Port Church was near at hand, and as the long procession turned out of Master Standfast's house, the June sunshine lay upon the bier, and as if seeking something bright in all that gloomy display, touched a lock of Margery's hair which had strayed from under the hood of her long mourning cloak, and made it shine like gold.

The two sisters walked behind the bent form of Master Standfast, who was chief mourner, and a long train of servants and apprentices brought up the rear; while the friends of the good merchant all sent some representative, as a token of respect to the living, perhaps, more than that of love for the dead. At the edge of the vault William Purdy came forward, and standing with uplifted hand prayed in that strange fashion of deprecation and appeal, rather than of praise and entreaty, which marked the Puritan acts of devotion. Regardless of the feelings of those around him, Will Purdy continued his prayer till every one felt wound up to the last pitch of endurance.

A strange, sad funeral it was, and the hearts of many were heavy as they saw the order of the Church they loved set aside, and the customs of their fathers rudely replaced by the unauthorised interference of a man like Will Purdy.

No one felt this state of things more keenly than Master William Colston, who stood with bowed head near his son, and was heard to murmur below his breath:

"Peace, enough! Lord, how long shall they wrest Thy Word to their own fancies, and leave Thy Church a wilderness?"

At last it was over, and the long file of mourners turned away from the open vault to Master Thomas Standfast's house; there a plentiful supply of biscuits and burnt claret was served by attendants in white gloves, and many friends sat down to it.

The "mockery of woe" indeed it seemed, as voices grew loud, and the conversation was a great contrast to the sombre dresses of the people gathered together.

To his closest friends Master Standfast presented a mourning ring, with the name and date of birth and death of his late wife engraved within; and some of a less expensive kind to others. All was done that was considered necessary to show respect to the dead, "a lady of quality," though no representatives of her own family were present. Damaris and Margery were excused from appearing after the return from church, and retired to their chamber at the top of the house. When the tread of many feet was hushed, and the servants had cleared away the remnants of the feast, giving a large quantity of fragments to the poor who thronged the street, Damaris crept down into the lower room to find her father.

He was seated in his large chair in the little room where he transacted business, his attitude one of extreme dejection rather than of poignant grief.

"Father," Damaris said, "this has been a hard day. Margery is worn out and has sought her pillow; will not you also go to rest?"

"Nay, child, not yet. I should not sleep; it's scarce sunset. I am thinking over the past, Damaris, Thy own mother seems near me, and thyself as a little child once more. The dear soul who is gone, had but little comfort in her life of late. God rest her soul. I have not done for her what I might. Ah, me! How is it, child, that when death cometh, and silence falls between us and the dead, up start all manner of laments, for sins against them. Ah, well-a-day, if I could see thee and thy young sister safely wedded I should be ready to depart. Is there no hope thereof, Damaris?"

"Dear father, no, not for me. Margery will most like find a husband. It is but to look on her, and a man is taken with her. See, for example, the gay young gentleman who went with us on the water that day—that day, a week agone, which seemeth like a year."

"He is not one I should covet to see bound to my daughter," Thomas Standfast said. "He is a bird of gay plumage, who is but a Will-o'-the-wisp. I hope Margery will not be taken by him. Master Edward Colston, now—"

"I do not deem he is like to fall in love with Margery," Damaris said, her cheek flushing crimson, "he is of too sober and quiet a nature; but there is no law in love-making."

"Nay, verily, thou art right, Damaris; to the end of time a fair outside will be a bait. But I do not think that Master William Colston would disapprove of a match between his son and one of you."

"Father," Damaris said, "you forget. I

am ten years older than Edward Colston, and such notions hurt me. I, who saw my betrothed lie before me dead, ere I had reached my eighteenth birthday! I have no heart for love."

Thomas Standfast sighed. "Well, well, thou art a good daughter to me, and thou rulest this poor stricken house wisely and well."

"I have a favour to ask of thee, dear father, concerning the household. Mother's old waiting-woman is over-aged and feeble. Methinks if she could find a place in the farm over by Stapleton, where Dame Pugsley sends the aged and poor, I should like to fill her place with a poor desolate child, Grace Goldsmith, who is in hiding at the top of Cicely Purdy's house. May I have her for my maid?"

"An it please you; but have a care you get into no trouble with any Quaker fanatic, Damaris."

"The girl has taken to me, and is amenable and gentle. I think if she be left to her own devices, she will lose her senses, and will languish and die in some dark cell. Her mother, who is verily half crazed, is shut up in a hole below Newgate, where scarce a dog could lie. Surely these things cry out for redress. How can it be pleasing to the Lord of love to see His creatures so treated for the sake of truth. In this city of Bristol how many aching hearts this day—how many tormented in prisons who are innocent? It seemeth to me that I could cry out at times, Hath God forgotten to be gracious?"

As Damaris spoke, her beautiful face, which was set off by her sombre garments, glowed with enthusiasm, and with her long white hands clasped together she said passionately, and as if with a prophetic inspiration—

"It is not so. He cannot forget, and there will be a light breaking through the darkness ere long. We shall see some great man raised up to care for Bristol—our dear city—and these time-servers will be made ashamed of themselves."

Thomas Standfast sighed. He could not follow his daughter in all her deep longings and higher aims; but, he said, as he looked at her, "Have a care, Damaris, or the fanatics will be making a proselyte of thee. Women must look to their households, and their kith and kin; it is not for them to meddle with public matters. There must be prisons for evil doers, and if folks are not law-abiding they must take the penalty. If thou must have this Grace Goldsmith, see to it that she behaves as a decent woman should. We suffer enow from Purdy's preachment, and we do not need a Quaker to confuse us more. Could'st bring me a posset, Damaris?" Thomas Standfast said, "hot and well spiced, for I am tired and cold, though it be a midsummer evening. I hope all was done in proper order at the funeral," he said. "Didst hear any adverse comments thereon?"

"No, dear father," Damaris said, putting her arm round the old man's neck, and kissing his forehead. "No; none could say that there was not due respect shown to our poor mother. Purdy's long preachment was the only matter that jarred on most folks. I saw Master Colston shrugging his shoulders."

"Aye, and well he might; but one might as lieve try to turn back the flow of yon river as stop his tongue. A good and trusty fellow in the business, and I must e'en put up with him. I am too old to change; my time is short."

Damaris went to prepare the posset for her

father, and found many poor people in the inner hall through the kitchen, eagerly looking for the broken fragments left from the funeral feast.

Many of the faces were wan and haggard, and bespoke extreme poverty. Damaris's stately figure moved here and there, filling the baskets and pipkins the people had brought. Blessings followed her, and she had a grave but kind word to say to many of them, especially to the poor children, who showed signs of neglect—both of body and mind. The children of the very poor in those times were but little considered, and their education had not entered into the mind of that mighty Corporation, who sat in solemn conclave in their municipal chamber to settle the affairs of their ancient city.

At this time the word 'loyal' could not be added. The council were all submissive servants of the Lord Protector, at whose behest a Fast-day was proclaimed for the first day of July, and met at nine o'clock to deliberate upon the best way of enforcing the command issued from Whitehall. Two years before, these worthy magistrates had, in obedience to the mandate of the 'ruling power,' ordered the destruction of their noble castle, which had seen the changes and chances of six centuries, and we read that every Alderman, or his deputy, was pledged to be present to encourage the work when the castle, the last strong defence of Bristol, was doomed to destruction. There seemed to be a general satisfaction in destroying the old landmarks at this time, and the Council-chamber at Bristol was foremost in its enthusiasm to carry out the work of destruction.

We may do well to contrast the figure of some portly member of the council in 1653, panting and puffing with importance as he scaled St. Michael's Hill, to watch the blows of pick-axe and crowbar, hailing with a cheer the rolling down of the old stones in a cloud of dust and mortar,—with the tall, spare form of Edward Colston, who, many years later, appeared amongst the men employed in building his great school-house. He was often seen, we are told, covered with dust and lime, turning a grindstone at a pinch, and scaling ladders, to encourage the workmen to diligence and speed, in the erection of one of the greatest monuments of his benevolence.

The first of July was an oppressive summer

day, without sunshine, and heavy skies. All business was suspended, and the Puritan ministers, who had taken the pulpits of the ordained clergy, were engaged in praying or preaching for seven hours.

No wonder poor little Dick and Joan Purdy looked forward to it with dread. It might be possible for the stalwart Dorothy Hassard—and my Lady Rogers, who though now bending under the weight of seventy years, was still vigorous and strong as in the old days—to keep up the religious excitement at high pressure through seven hours of prayers and sermons; but it was hard for the children to maintain a demure and unwearied aspect through the long, long hours.

Damaris and Margery, in their long black mourning cloaks and hoods, went to St. Mary le Port; but Margery's patience failed, for during the pause in which the minister retired to refresh himself, though the people continued singing, she slipped away, and at the door was met by Master Hyacinth Sacheverell.

He took off his plumed cap and bowed low. They had not met since the day of the water party, for Hyacinth had no taste for the house of mourning.

"May I crave leave to escort you home, Mistress Margery?" he said; adding, "it grieves me to see the evening star of beauty veiled in dark clouds."

Margery had been unused to compliments so well turned, and uttered in a low, silvery voice:

"Thanks, sir," she said; "these have been dark, long days, and to crown them all, this Fast-day! I cannot abide the service a minute longer. I have left Damaris, who can pray all day and not weary; and I am sure she is welcome."

Master Hyacinth Sacheverell had been a little doubtful whether he might not find the fair Margery grief-struck for her mother's loss; but the tone was re-assuring, and he offered her his hand, to guide her across several unseemly heaps of refuse which lay in the way, and they turned into the shadow of Mary le Port Street together.

A man was keeping watch in the gloomy hall; and old Hannah came to the top of the stairs to see who was returning.

"Aye, then, Margery," she exclaimed, "so you've cut short the Fast service; like your blessed mother, you do not suit well with darkness and gloom, and right too; youth is your time, and it's good to leave aches and pains of heart and body for old creatures like me. For I miss my poor lady, and feel I ain't long for this world. Time I went, when a cracked Quaker girl is brought in."

Thus talking in a garrulous fashion, old Hannah walked into the large room before Margery and Master Hyacinth, and asked if she should bring some cordial and comfits from her cupboard.

"Yes, Hannah, that's a good thought. Methinks neither Master Hyacinth nor I wish to live on bread and water, Fast-day though it be."

"Nay, indeed," said Master Hyacinth, greatly relieved to find that he had not to deal with a sorrow-struck daughter who was mourning for her mother. He made the best of his time, and talked and chattered in the easy-going fashion of a gallant of those days. He was altogether so widely different from the few men whom Margery had ever seen, that she was quite captivated by him. He threw himself in a graceful attitude on a settle, and watched the varying expression of her face, as he told her stories of the great world, and of the glories of the past, when his mother was about the court of the Queen Henrietta Maria. I will not say that the stories were all true, or that Master Hyacinth did not colour them with his own imagination. But they served their purpose, and Margery was a good listener, and believed all he told her to be trustworthy.

"I am come hither," he said, "just to bide my time. My father, like all good Royalists, suffered greatly from the triumph of these rebels, and his estate was confiscated; so I am constrained to take to trade. He is a merchant, but different from these city magnates. He had a footing as well in the county, and a fine house and retainers. All this is past; but when the king has his own again we shall recover our lost property, and then—"

"Then you will be grand folk, and look down on city merchants," Margery said.

"Nay, methinks such merchants as we see in Bristol are princes of the earth, and their daughters queens."

"My mother," said Margery, innocently accepting the compliment, "my mother came of a noble house—the FitzHardinges—while Damaris's mother was but the daughter of a soap-boiler in St. Peter's Square."

"Ah! I could have sworn you had gentle blood in your veins. Your sister has the dignity of a Lady Abbess. Can she ever laugh?"

"Oh yes, Damaris can be gay; on occasions she is full of humour: but you must know her lover, young Will Pugsley, fell in one of the cruel fights years agone, and Damaris has never been the same again. She has had nought to do with other lovers since then, and will never marry."

Hyacinth stroked his heavy curls, and said,

"I warrant some fine gentleman will change her resolve some day. Well-a-day, fair Mistress Margery, you have turned the Fast-day into a feast. But I must away. I hear steps below —some of the household returning from the preachments;" and, kneeling, he kissed Margery's hand and departed, leaving her in a flutter of a new joy, which was shining on her face when Damaris returned from church. Damaris was very tired, and glad to throw herself into a chair, while Margery unfastened her cloak and hood, and, bending over her, kissed her.

"Damaris, why did you stay so long listening to Master Eames, who is no more fit to preach than an old cat? I'd had enow, and came home to change my fast for a feast, so Master Hyacinth Sacheverell called it. Oh! Damaris, he is brave and grand to look at, and turns such fine speeches, and tells such stories of the court before these bad times came upon the land."

"Be not too much taken with fair speeches, Margery; methinks it ill becomes you to talk so gaily, and our poor mother but lately buried. Life is but as a dream, Margery, and all flesh as grass. Why, it seemeth but yesterday that I stood here a little maiden, and saw poor mother in all her brave attire come in from Edward Colston's christening feast. And now to think on it all. The mother stricken in the dread plague, her beauty consumed away like a moth, though her life was spared. All her beauteous gowns and ornaments—what are they now—now that she is hidden from all eyes in the dark vault? Sweet sister, there are better things to crave after, than aught that the world gives."

Margery was a little touched by her sister's earnest tones.

"I don't want to be hard-hearted. I am sorry for poor mother; but oh! Damaris, it is nice to be young and to be loved"—she pronounced the word timidly. "What if Master Hyacinth could and did love me?"

"Child, do not be taken by a few soft words. If it were Master Edward Colston now—"

Margery laughed scornfully.

"As if a solemn, slow man like Master Colston could ever love! I'd as lieve marry Master Eames. But," with a toss of her pretty head, "I may wait till I am asked, though it seems to me that Master Edward of the sober face would fain win thy favour."

The deepest rose-colour flushed Damaris's cheek, as she rose and said:

"Hush; nor prate so idly, Margery, Edward Colston is a boy, and I am a woman. Now I must see to my poor Grace;" and Damaris put out her hand to steady herself.

"I am giddy from the fast. Methinks I must break it now," and she took the silver flagon which old Hannah had brought in for Master Sacheverell and put it to her lips, and breaking a bit of the funeral cake eat it eagerly.

"Forsooth you are famished — starving, Damaris. What folly! If the fasting would bring back the king, I'd fast for a day, perchance," Margery exclaimed. "But where is the use of fasting till you are sick, for nought?"

"I am not sick; it was but a passing sense

of giddiness;" and Damaris went slowly from the room.

Many formal visits of condolence were paid to Thomas Standfast's family.

The wives and daughters of the merchants who had borne poor Mistress Standfast but scant good will in her life, now came with the doleful air that was thought becoming, and nibbled the richly-spiced biscuits, and sipped the burnt claret, which was placed on a sideboard, and talked of the loss the girls had sustained, and the uncertainty of life. The Lady Rogers came in her chair, carried by four attendants, and looked with a keen, faultfinding eye, round the room; asked what were the intentions of the two sisters as to household matters now their mother was gone, and rebuked Margery for suffering her golden hair to stray over her black dress.

"In deep mourning it should be shorn or tucked up, methinks," said Lady Rogers.

Mistress Dorothy Hassard also came, stout and stalwart as of old; age had not broken her spirit, or slackened the vehemence of her tongue. Her second husband, mild and gentle in voice and manner, stood somewhat in awe of his wife, who had once led a valiant troop of women to defend the city gates, and had found it her wifely duty to leave the church where he ministered, because he "bowed the knee to Baal."

All this was long past now; but Dorothy still looked able to hold her own against a troop, and to be full of fervour for the cause, as she believed it, of right and truth.

Strange it was—or it would be strange, did we not see the same spirit abroad in our own and every time—that Dorothy, the most devoted woman of the Puritan community in Bristol, was the most vehement in her hatred of the Quakers. A rumour had reached her that Grace Goldsmith had been concealed by Cicely Purdy, and she now stalked across the courtyard to rate her soundly for so doing, denouncing George Fox and his followers as stirrers up of strife, and "empty-headed coxcombs," who believed only in themselves, and despised others.

Cicely Purdy had long ago learned the golden rule of silence; she had need to do so, or Will Purdy would have made her life a burden to her. So she took Mistress Hassard's tirade very quietly, merely saying she had sheltered the defenceless girl, and protected her from the rude crowd which had pursued and assaulted her, and she would do so again.

"And turn Quaker if necessary, and rave and rant, and walk in a hair shirt, to the shame of all decent folk, through Bristol streets!"

"The poor mother," Cicely said, "is distraught, doubtless: but she pays a bitter penalty, left to languish in a loathsome dungeon in Newgate."

"Ah, ha!" said Mistress Hassard, "you have learned your lesson well, and taught it to the daughters of Master Standfast, doubtless. Is that maiden in thy house now, Cicely?"

"No, verily; she hath left my care," said Cicely quietly.

And then Mistress Hassard, defeated at all points, though maintaining the air of the conqueror, marched away to bestow spiritual consolation on the two sisters in Thomas Standfast's house.

Mistress Colston came also, with her sweet maternal tenderness and overflowing sympathy, and the beautiful and gracious widow from Nugent Hill, Dame Joanna Pugsley, between whom and Damaris there existed a strong tie.

Damaris was thankful to be alone when the tall graceful figure of her friend, clothed in her long black garments of widowhood, came with a slow, stately movement into the room. She held out her arms to Damaris, and the two were locked in a long embrace.

"I should have been hither before," Dame Pugsley said, "but I have had so many sick to tend, and I have been thinking sadly of the past. These twelve years since that dread day do seem so dream-like to me, and I have been worried with a suitor the last week. As if I could be the wife of any other but him whose wife I am to all eternity. Thy mother, did she suffer much at the end? Dear Damaris, I am sure you have passed through deep waters."

"Yes;" Damaris said, "not so much of personal loss, for the poor mother had so long been astray in her mind; but there was a ray of hope and light at the last, and there was no pain. But oh! methinks life going out thus is a sadder sight than when in all the vigour of manhood or womanhood it is given gladly for a righteous cause."

Dame Pugsley put her arm round Damaris. "Ah!" she said, "I feel your words to be true. Often when I think of my young hero falling in the fight, I say the beauteous memory of his courage and devotion to his King and his country, can never be dimmed, and that in all the surging floods of unrest, and faction, and rebellion, and the triumph of the great mover thereof in high places, I rejoice that my husband is safe in the highest. No fall for him; no temptation to cringe to the powers that be—wrongfully the powers. And then I feel contentment—not joy, not gladness—but peace. But, Damaris, come up to the Hill and tarry a few days. I have much to show you there. I have a scheme for gathering some of the maidens about me into a school for work, and their mothers I hope to have also for comfort; for there are many sore hearts which bear about a daily burden, and we women can comfort one another, if we set about it aright."

"You have the power to do so," Damaris said. "I must not leave the household at present, Margery needeth an elder sister's hand over her—"

"What! hath a young gentleman come on the scene?"

"Aye, indeed, and a gay one. Hark! I hear steps on the stairs," and Damaris answered the tap at the door to admit Edward Colston.

He had been slow to intrude himself in the house of mourning; he was always reserved, and he knew he had not the easy manner of many of his young contemporaries.

Damaris greeted him warmly, and set him more at ease, introducing him formally to Dame Pugsley, adding, "This is my friend, Master Colston, of whom I spoke to you as constant in good deeds, and care for the learning of the poor children."

Edward Colston made one of his stiff bows, and stood, till Damaris said, "Dame Pugsley would fain, I know, that you were seated." But Edward Colston continued standing, saying that he had but ventured to come to inquire how Mistress Damaris and Mistress Margery did after their affliction, and that he would not disturb the conference he had interrupted.

"Nay, now," Dame Pugsley said turning her sweet serious face towards Edward Colston, "we can afford to be interrupted for we meet often. Tell me, Master Colston, how your good father does, and your mother. Your father and I have a strong tie between us, and I wish he would oftener seek me out."

"He fears to trespass on your time, lady, perchance; but I am a stranger in my native city, nor have I visited it since I was a boy, therefore I did not even know that my father had the honour of your acquaintance."

"Ah, I forgot he told me once his eldest-borr was at school, away from him. These twelve years of which I was speaking to Damaris, are a large part of your life. But your good father proved brave as a soldier in that troubled time, and stood out valiantly against the rebels; though methinks his victory was even greater on the day that he shook off the dust of his feet as he left the Council-chamber of traitorous rebels, or half-hearted friends. Your father's is a name ever to be held in honour; may you prove worthy to bear it."

These words of warm praise of his father touched Edward Colston's heart. He lingered long to listen to the conversation that followed between Damaris and her guest; and some words from them, as to the loving service which is a sign and badge of all Christian fellowship, fell like good seed in the young man's heart, to bring forth fruit abundantly in after years.

Edward Colston seemed from that day to have broken down the barrier of reserve between himself and Damaris. He often found his way to Mary le Port Street, and would sometimes escort the two sisters to his mother's house, where Mistress Sarah Colston always bade them welcome. Master Hyacinth Sacheverell was somewhat fitful in his attentions; sometimes he would be continually finding an excuse to come to Mary le Port Street, and to Master Colston's house, where he might meet the two sisters, and then several weeks would pass over and he would not appear.

He found more congenial companions than Edward Colston, in the sons of some of the Bristol merchants, who, though outwardly obliged to conform to their fathers' political and religious forms, and creeds, were at heart Royalists—if by Royalist we understand longing for freedom from all restraint and a return to a gay, unthinking life of pleasure and gaiety. For in this time of transition there seemed to be a general drifting away from old landmarks, and a strong current bearing down the people on its troubled waters, whither or wherefore the great majority neither knew nor cared. The sons of the rich and wealthy were chafed by the shackles of a new faith, which made a walk on Sunday a breach of the law, and imposed on them conditions which they evaded continually either openly or by craft, and they cared for very little beyond the selfish gratification of the desires of the moment and longed for the time when pleasures, now forbidden should be once more allowed.

Hence it was that the great restraint forced upon the people in the time of Cromwell's rule, when removed, had the most disastrous effects on the nation. It is always so; if the rein is pulled too tightly the horse will chafe and resent the bridle, and start off, as soon as it is slackened, in the contrary direction. Deeply, indeed, have nations and individuals reason to mourn over the after effects of a bigoted and undue restriction, put upon those who are only forced, and not led, and therefore hasten to escape from their trammels at the first opportunity.

Edward Colston and Damaris exchanged many opinions about Master Sacheverell, and Damaris could not fail to notice a change in Margery.

She was merry and sad, good-tempered and cross by turns; and Damaris saw that her bright days were always those when Master Hyacinth had been devoting himself to her, and the gloomy ones those when he was absent.

"Were I her mother," Damaris said, "I would ask Master Hyacinth what he means by this dallying; but I shrink from it, like a coward."

Damaris made this remark to Edward Colston as they sat together on a bench in the Bullock Park on a golden September evening.

"I dare not ask him," she said again, as she watched Margery walking to and fro with the gay Master Sacheverell, and was not slow to perceive that grave and disapproving looks were cast upon her by some of her neighbours, who were seated on the benches facing her, for the Park was much resorted to in fine weather by the wives and daughters of the Bristol citizens.

Edward Colston became suddenly absorbed with the hilt of his short sword, and made no rejoinder. Damaris felt almost vexed with herself that she had said anything which might seem to imply that her sister was to blame in accepting attentions which apparently had no real meaning, and said hastily:

"True love is so beautiful, it irks me to see the counterfeit."

"Yes," Edward Colston said, "true love must be God's best gift; but where to seek for it now-a-days?"

"Oh! it lives in spite of storms and tempests," said Damaris. "See how Dame Pugsley is true to her early love. She keepeth sacred all things that belonged to him. She has his coat pierced with the sabre cuts and drenched with his life blood; she preserves them as relics, and her wedding gown is to be her shroud. See her, beautiful and rich, living in widowhood for his sake. Do not tell me love is dead; it must ever live, for its root lies too deep to perish; the garish weeds which mock it by a seeming likeness may die, but *not* true love."

"It hath a warm defender in you," said Edward Colston.

"Aye, and in your mother also: how beautiful is her care of and devotion to your father, who, like mine, looks more aged every day. Our kinsman, Richard Standfast, who is one of the sufferers whose livings are sequestrated by these unrighteous decrees, was with us yester even. Methinks that he looks on my dear father's condition as a fast failing one, and when he is gone—ah, me! my heart sinks to say that word—my life will be desolate, and I fancy Will Purdy, who has so greatly gained the ascendancy over my father, will rule us, or try to rule us with a heavy hand."

"There will be friends to stand out against that, methinks," Edward Colston said, with sudden warmth. "Damaris, I must speak, and yet I know not how you will receive what I tell you. I pray you, be not disdainful or turn your head away, or I shall never get through what I have to say."

Damaris could not resist a smile at this lengthy preface, to what she half dreaded, yet half longed to hear. For there is no true woman, to whom the love of any good man is not in some sort acceptable. She may not be able to respond to it, or she may feel that she cannot do so; but a true woman can never treat the love of a good man lightly, and she must always feel a certain sense of honour done her, by the avowal which, from all sorts of misconceptions, is often held back till too late.

"I am to depart for Spain in the next month; before I go I must speak. From the first moment of my return and meeting you, Damaris, I have loved you."

"As a sister," she hastily interrupted; "as a sister older than yourself."

"Nay, nay, no sister-love is this. You speak of age. I am in all my thoughts and ways older than you are. It is as my wife I would fain love you. Oh! Damaris, say not nay, I beseech you."

"Dear friend," said Damaris, "I ought to have avoided this. I fear I have been to blame. Your friendship has been very sweet to me, and we see alike in so many things; but to promise to be your wife—ah! no. I should be wrong, indeed, to promise what would work ill for you."

"It would work well for me for time and eternity. Methinks you know not what you do by refusing this earnest prayer of mine. Is it that your heart, like your friend's, is buried with your first love?"

"I would not deceive you or any man, Edward Colston; I would not say that the loss of my young lover in that fearful fight is the sole reason why I never mean to wed. But leaving that, I come to good reasons. A young man of twenty-one must not seek for a wife of thirty. On your return from Spain you will find me with grey hair and an old woman."

"Damaris, I say age hath nought to do with this. I love you with all my soul, and," he added solemnly, "I could love no other. I count not years, I do not acknowledge their power. You are to me in all the prime and beauty of womanhood, fairer than any woman ever was or could be; but it is not only this;

methinks that you and I could do something together for the poor folk of our native city. I see a bright future before me with you, without you, a cold drear journey, which may be long or short as God pleases, but will never know another love."

"Oh," Damaris exclaimed, touched by his earnestness and evident sincerity, "if only you had looked upon Margery instead of me, what joy in place of the grief this love for me must bring you!"

"Margery! Edward Colston exclaimed. "Ah! think you not I have heard of this before? My father has mooted the subject to me, and there have been others who have thought I might woo and win that gay laughing creature. But my mother knows my heart, and she is full of sympathy with me. Oh, let me show you what a life's devotion can do."

"Methinks," said Damaris, with a sad smile, "you are a witness that true and disinterested love is still alive in these days, and thus stand a contradiction to yourself."

He caught at hope from these words, and said, eagerly—

"Oh, Damaris, you will not send me empty away? I feel as if the warm springs would be for ever closed in my heart if you will not let them flow for you. Let us show what two lives united might do for God and our fellow-creatures. Damaris, say that you will relent."

How beautiful her face looked in the golden light of the western sunshine, as Edward Colston gazed on it. It was illuminated with the soft radiance of a saint or angel in the window of a church Edward Colston dimly recalled as a memory of his boyhood. There was high resolve written on it, and tenderness, and love; but not for him. Ah! not for him. Then, after a minute's pause, she rose, and leaving him seated, said:

"I cannot be your wife, Edward, but I am your friend while life lasts; and I know well when you are wedded to one of your own age, and worthy of you, you will still count me as a friend, and would serve me, if the need arose, faithfully as a friend, aye, and lovingly as a brother might!"

The light of hope died out of Edward Colston's face. He saw his fate was sealed. The old stiff reserve crept over him again, as he said, rising and bowing low:

"Be it so, Mistress Damaris. I will be your friend—to serve you well if the need arise."

"Or those I love, Edward," she said. "Am I asking too much, for my heart is sore troubled for Margery?"

"I will serve you, or those you love, with my best endeavours—with my life's blood, if need be; with all my worldly substance, if so it fall out. Rest in this assurance from a heart pierced deep with a life-wound by your dear hand."

Then, taking one of Damaris' slender white hands in his, Edward Colston pressed it to his lips fervently, and turned and left her.

A light laugh smote upon his ear as he passed a bench in a retired corner of the Park. It was Margery's laugh—the little silvery ripple which answered Hyacinth's soft speeches.

"Whither away, Master Colston, in such haste, and leaving your lady-love alone, with scant courtesy?" exclaimed Hyacinth.

"Peace," said Edward Colston, angrily; "verily your laughter is as the crackling of thorns under a pot."

"A right good Puritan quotation; we'll have thee in the Quaker's garb ere long."

Edward Colston strode away, but Damaris crossed the turf, and standing before her sister and Hyacinth said:

"The evening is drawing in, Margery; most folks have left the Park. It is not well to linger."

"So Edward Colston thought. Fie, then, Damaris, for sending him off, like a beaten hound."

"Margery!" and in that single word, with flashing eyes and proud contempt, Damaris implied more than by a longer string of merited reproofs. Margery was silenced, and Hyacinth rising, said:

"Yes, forsooth, Mistress Damaris is right. The public ways are not too seemly for fair ladies to be abroad at dusk." And even as he spoke there was a sound of a noisy throng, above which might be heard a man's voice in a sing-song monotone.

"One of the Quakers holding forth," Hyacinth continued. "They have some spirit for outward things as well as the inward spirit they speak so much of: they face sticks and stones and rotten eggs in a manner truly edifying."

As he spoke a young man was seen, with a little band of followers, raised on a heap of stones, crying out that the Spirit of the Lord was upon him, and that he was commissioned to pull down the strongholds of the steeple-houses, and bid the dumb dogs come down from high places.

Instantly there rose a loud chorus of barking and hooting, and cries of "Pull him down!"

"Ah!" exclaimed Damaris, "what mean those cravens to set on a defenceless man! Cannot you speak—cannot *you*, a man, do aught?" She took Hyacinth by the sleeve of his velvet tunic as if to detain him.

"They turn this way," he exclaimed. "We shall get into the rout; and a pretty thing, indeed, that will be for two fair ladies."

He hurried them by another by-lane at the back of the cathedral, and coming out by St. Augustine's church they got into comparative quiet, and were soon at Thomas Standfast's house in Mary le Port Street.

When Edward Colston left Damaris he walked quickly in the direction of his own house. He scarcely knew how much he had loved Damaris till he knew too surely it was hopeless to win her love in return. His heart was heavy with a dull sense of misery, for which he could as yet think of no relief. The noise of the rabble crowd pursuing the Quaker reached him from afar, but he hardly heeded it. He could see before him nothing but the face he loved, illuminated by the golden light of the sunset sky, and he wondered whether along all life's pathway that face would be present with him as now—beautiful, holy in its wistful gaze, but always far off—never, never near him again. As he passed one of the many city churches, the clock above chimed seven. The doors were open, for some demolition of popish images and carving had been going on there by order of the Presbyterian minister, who had supplanted the lawful incumbent of the living. Edward Colston turned in, and saw a man and woman busily engaged in sweeping up the chips and dust, with which the work of demolition had strewed the aisles.

The woman paused in her work, and leaning on her broom, looked at him. He walked up to the east end of the church with his slow and stately tread, unusual in a man so young, and looked sadly at the mischief which had been wrought there. This was the church where, after a dim fashion, he remembered as a boy, the face in the painted glass window in a little side chapel. He sought it, not with any certainty of finding it, but with a sort of instinctive idea that it was here. The chapel was a family burial-place of some of the Berkeleys, and the small lancet-shaped window was above the monument of a knight and his lady, carved in stone below it.

The chapel had escaped the general demolition of the body of the church, and there, catching the light of the daffodil sky behind it, was the face. The same which, looking out into the sunset, had an hour before become dearer than ever to him—and hopelessly dear.

As Edward Colston gazed at the face in the window a mist rose before his eyes, and ere he was aware of it, large tears fell upon his velvet coat. He followed the natural impulse of most young hearts in trouble, and kneeling, covered his face with his hands and prayed—that voiceless, wordless prayer which the stricken ones of every age and time have felt to be a comfort, as bringing near to the soul the Helper of the helpless.

After a few minutes' silence Edward Colston was aware that there were voices behind him.

"A poor popish cretur'," said the woman's voice; while the man gave Edward Colston a warning tap with a stick on his shoulder.

"We are closing the place"—he did not say church. "Methinks, unless you choose to bide all night, you must depart, my young sir."

Rising from his knees with a stately inclination of his head, Colston passed out of the chapel, turning once more to look at the face in the window. As he did so he heard the man say:

"A fine gentleman, forsooth, and never a doit to the poor!"

Edward Colston put his hand into his pocket and drawing out a piece of silver, he dropped it into the man's hand.

"Bless you, my good young gentleman; if you came to see the winder in the chapel you ain't too soon. They be going to break it up to-morrow, for there's some popish words under it in the glass—terrible popish words, so they say."

Edward Colston returned, and descending the two worn stone steps into the chapel, read what he had overlooked before.

"Poor ignorant souls," he said; "who can lay blame to them?" And the lips of that sweet face seemed almost to open in reply and repeat the words, "Expecto vitam venturi sæculi."

When Edward Colston reached his house in Small Street, his two young brothers were in the wide hall. Evidently they were talking together of something of importance.

"Heigh, Ned!" the younger one called; "there is news."

"News!" said Edward, dreamily. "Well, what news?"

"Bad news, as we think. Our father has been closeted with the messenger from London Docks for a long time. I caught one of the clerks, and he said, 'Ill news, indeed. The *Society of Bristol* is taken by the rascally Spaniards.'"

Edward seemed to wake now to the reality of his brother's announcement.

"The *Society of Bristol* taken! It had a large cargo of wine and oil. The loss will be great. Where is our mother, Robert?"

"In her chamber with little Mall, who is ailing. She knows nought of this."

"Then keep it from her till I have seen my father; as see him I must."

And now Edward Colston, like many of us, experienced the benefit of a lesser trial coming to brace us to bear the greater. For what was the loss of the good ship the *Society of Bristol* when compared with the loss of Damaris? What were the wine and the oil when put in the balance with the love and sweet graciousness of her who was to him the queen amongst women. But now he must throw aside this great weight of care, and rise to the help and comfort of his old father. He crossed the spacious hall, and turned to the large door of his father's business room, with its carved staple and Colston arms on a shield above it.

"Methought he had heard the news," said Thomas, the younger of the two brothers, "he looked so grim and melancholy."

"He never looks much else," Robert returned; "his gravity might become three-score years."

Edward Colston knocked at the door, and was admitted at once. His father was seated at the head of a long table, and several friends and neighbours were gathered round him. The letter brought by a special messenger in his saddle-bags from London lay open on the table, and when William Colston saw his son he pointed to it, and said:

"Read the story of ruin, my son; you are of age; judge for yourself. It concerneth me less than my sons. Do not grieve unduly for the losses of one whose time is short."

"Nay, nay, say not so," said Master Aldworth, of St. Peter's, who was involved to some small extent in the loss. "Nay, you have many

OLD SUGAR HOUSE IN ST. PETER'S CHURCHYARD.
Now the property of the Corporation of the Poor.

good years before you. We cannot spare you from us."

William Colston shook his head. "My friend Thomas Standfast and I are fast going down hill, and we know it." The two men, with a sudden impulse, stretched their hands out to each other, and they met in a strong clasp.

"You are far behind me in the race, Master Colston," said Thomas Standfast, "and you have good sons to be your help; while I have but two girls, whom it goes hard to leave in this cold world."

Edward Colston, who had been reading the letter, looked up quickly. He was now for the first time conscious that the father of Damaris was present.

A large fire was burning on the wide hearth, and sent fitful shadows on the richly carved panels of the room, and threw out the figures of the merchants in strong relief. Edward Colston stood a little apart, nearer the window, where the twilight yet lingered, and was sufficient to enable his young eyes to decipher the writing of the letter, which ran thus—

"To our good and trusty friend and fellow-merchant, Master William Colston, of Small Street, Bristol.

"It grieveth me sore, right worthy sir, to convey to you tidings which have reached us this day from the port of Alicant in the kingdom of Spain, to the effect that the good ship named in the deeds of freightage the *Society of Bristol*, laden with a goodly cargo of wine of the choicest, and olive oil, was seized by a troop of ill-disposed piratical Spaniards, and her cargo sold by them. Her captain, William Hall, and her crew, left with the skin of their teeth to tell the tale of woe to your agent at Alicant, who has signified the same to me by letters conveyed by a craft bound from Alicant, and sailing three days after the loss was reported.

"Worthy sir, I pray you to receive my condolence, and hope that we may gain redress by punishing of the villains.

"With the respectful greeting of your servant,

"JOSEPH HALL,

"First cousin on the mother's side to William Hall, late Captain of the *Society of Bristol*."

The scene was one for a painter's brush as Edward Colston advanced to the table after reading the letter.

"It is ill tidings, but your fortune, my father, rests not wholly with the cargo of the *Society of Bristol*. It seemeth to me, good gentlemen, that my departure for Spain can no longer be delayed, and that it is my duty as my pleasure, to take ship from this port with all haste, and discover, if God grant me a good voyage, whether I may do aught to retrieve the loss. Be not down-hearted, father, I will do my best to serve and help you."

The old men collected in the room could not resist a murmur of applause, but William Colston, with a face in which paternal pride triumphed over the shadows of care and anxiety, said :

"God be with you, my son, and speed you on your way, and prosper you a hundredfold for your goodness to me in my declining years. I commission you to seek your mother, and tell her if she have lost a fortune she hath gained a double share of a woman's heritage in the love of a dutiful son."

"Aye, verily," said Thomas Standfast; "happy mother to possess such a son as you are, Edward Colston. She can never be poor."

"Father," said Edward Colston, before leaving the room to seek his mother, "with your leave I will send in my two younger brothers to hear your wishes, and if I might advise, it would be that they are now of an age to be treated with your confidence, and that they might also do good service to you in the distant country where the wide spread of your mercantile transactions renders supervision increasingly needful."

"Well said," was the father's answer; "let the boys be called."

As Edward Colston passed out to seek his mother, he told the two young brothers that they were to go in and hear of their father's troubles, and he added,

"Quit you like men, boys, and do your part to serve him and console him."

"Aye, that we will, Ned; and now go to our mother, she has feared something is wrong, for little Will has been downstairs twice to ask if the gentlemen were gone, and if you were at hand."

Edward Colston went up the wide staircase, and passing the first flight, reached the second, where his mother slept. Like all the rooms in this spacious house, of one of the greatest of Bristol merchants, it was large, but, as we should think now, very insufficiently lighted. The windows were large latticed bays, it is true, high above the oak panels, but they were raised some five feet from the floor, and were not the projecting bays, as on the lower story, but tall, with two lights ending in a trefoil at the top.

The room was dark even at noon, and now in the evening shadows it was difficult to discern any object clearly. But before the wood fire, Edward Colston saw the outline of his mother's figure as she sat in a low chair with little Mall on her knee.

Will came forward and said, "Hush, brother Ned, Mall sleeps."

The boy's words made Sarah Colston turn, and she could see in the dim light her eldest son's tall figure advancing towards her.

"You have come to tell me the news, Edward. A rumour has reached me by the maidens that thy father is in sore trouble. Little Mall is sound asleep at last. I will lay her on the bed, and then I can better hear what you have to tell."

"Mother," said little Will, who had been left, as he considered, on guard by his two elder brothers, "mother, now Ned has come, prythee, let me run down to Doll, and have a cake and a drink of milk."

"Aye, surely, dear boy. I had forgot how time passed, and thou must need thy supper, and then to bed; and, Will, see that no one disturbs me till I call. I have much to say to, and hear from, brother Ned."

"A second Edward," the mother said tenderly, after having put Mall to bed; "he is so full of thought at his tender years. Now, then, tell me; is it great loss of fortune, and how does thy father bear it, if so it is?"

"The good ship, the *Society of Bristol*, was taken by robber Spaniards, and the cargo—a very valuable one—sold."

"Well," said Sarah Colston, "well, dear son, if such is the loss, it is heavy and grievous; but it is nought, if thy father bears up."

"He will bear up for thy sweet sake, mother. I am to hasten my departure for Spain, and the boys are to follow."

"Ah," said Sarah Colston, putting her hand to her side; "there is the pain—parting from thee and thy young brothers."

"But, mother, we knew it was to come; and coming sooner by a month or two is nought to weep over. It is well for me to go—*best* for me to go—for here I could not tarry."

The mother's ear caught the ring of heart-pain in her son's voice.

"Hast thou a trouble—a trouble apart from this of thy father's, dear son?"

Edward did not answer. He had been standing, with his back leaning against the high carved oak shelf over the open hearth, but now he left his position, and came near his mother, and kneeling down by her, he laid his head on her shoulder.

"Edward, my son, what is the trouble?" she asked, putting her arm round him tenderly, and kissing his bowed head. "Can I help you, my son?"

But Edward was still silent; he was bracing himself to speak calmly, and not betray too much of his sore heart to his mother.

"Dost remember, mother, that when I returned hither, three months agone, thou didst ask me if I had no lady of my love—no daughter in prospect to give you?"

"Yes, dear son, I remember," Mistress Colston said. "Is it really to be that my wish is fulfilled?"

"Nay, mother; it is, indeed, never to be fulfilled. I found that my whole heart was laid at the feet of—"

The name seemed as if it would not leave his lips, and his mother, pressing her face close to his, said in a low voice,

"Of Damaris Standfast, Edward?"

"Ah, yes; it could be no other! But now there must be silence respecting her henceforth. She will not listen to my suit; she rejects me wholly as her husband, and my heart is dead within me."

"Nay, my son, do not speak thus. Thy heart is full of youth and hope. Thou art but a boy, dear Edward. Thy time will come. And perhaps it is well, for she is thy senior, and—"

"Dear mother, I can only look at two things: I love her, and my love is vain. No years, or time, or circumstance can change me; and, dear mother, let there be silence henceforth between us on this matter. The future may bring me strong ties, though never those of wife and child; and while I have thee, sweet mother, I cannot be alone!"

"And thou hast One whose love is higher than mine, Edward; and when I am taken from thee, it will e'en be thy strength and support. God comfort thee and bless thee, my dear son, and shower on thy head His best blessings."

Then there was silence, during which the mother's heart was ascending to God in fervent longing for her first-born; while in his, the pain of Damaris's rejection of his love, was softened by the comfort of his mother's, which seemed to wrap him in a mantle of tenderness and warmth.

Ah, how blessed and beautiful is maternal love! Who shall measure its height, or sound its depth? Who shall say how many a wanderer has been reclaimed by the memory of that love, as it encompassed him in childhood, and was the atmosphere in which he lived? Not always, perhaps, felt and understood as Edward Colston felt it, in young manhood; but coming over the waste of years like a breath of pure air, to invigorate the soul when the burden and heat of life's day is heavy and toilsome.

From out the past, the voice of mothers like Sarah Colston seems to cry to the mothers of to-day, to be the friend of their sons, and to fulfil the high mission which God has given them as the "mother of boys." Patience, untiring love, unfailing forgiveness to the seventy times and seven, all knit together by the band of wisdom and judgment, for which mothers need to pray, and the mother is secure of her ground. Whatever sin or sorrow may come over the man's life, the memory of such a mother will be as a beacon pointing him to the ways of pleasantness and peace, of which she told him in his early days.

Alas! for the mother who allows the claims of

society, or art, or literature, or even of so-called charity itself, to come between her and her boy. She, of all others, should be at leisure from herself to hear of all his work at school—his games, his troubles there. She, of all others, should be ready to listen with a sympathetic ear, to throw in a word here, and a word there, of praise or blame, and to let her boy feel that from the least to the most important event of his life she takes a loving heart-interest. It is impossible not to look with sadness on the many mothers of these times who, immersed in the round of pleasure or the requirements of a conventional life, leave their children very much to themselves, and if they provide everything supposed to be suitable for their maintenance in the way of clothes and education, consider they have done their part. Alas! for the sons and daughters of such mothers; and not less may we say, alas! for the mothers themselves, who miss the great joy and blessedness of a woman's life!

Damaris was very much disinclined for Master Hyacinth Sacheverell's light jests at the supper-table. The absence of Thomas Standfast caused his daughter some anxiety, and as the time went on and he did not appear, she sent a message to William Purdy to inquire if he knew aught of his master.

But Will Purdy was also out, and Damaris heard one of the apprentices say in an undertone:

"Most like they're at Master Colston's in Small Street."

"Why think you so?" Damaris asked, turning to the apprentice. "I pray you conceal nothing."

"There is nought to conceal, lady, save that the news of the loss of the *Society of Bristol*, with all her rich cargo, is abroad in the city, and my master may have gone to learn the truth from Master Colston himself."

As he spoke Thomas Standfast was seen entering the hall leaning on Purdy's arm for support. He sank heavily into the large carved oaken chair at the head of the board, and Damaris was at his side in an instant.

She held a large silver tankard to her father's lips, and said:

"What troubles you, father?"

"My friends' troubles are mine," he replied. "Master Colston has lost what would ruin a poorer man, my daughter, but he has too much to fall back upon to be altogether ruined. Still it is a heavy blow—a mighty heavy blow."

"It is the hand of the Lord," snarled Will Purdy; "it is a token of His judgment against mammon worship and idol worship. The Colstons are surely known as—"

"As the best and noblest of men." It was Damaris's voice that rang out, not loud but clear, and Will Purdy, refusing a seat at the board, retired to his house across the courtyard, and gave Cicely the benefit of his denunciation upon the mammon worshippers of the day.

Long after Damaris had gone to her chamber she heard the voices of Hyacinth Sacheverell and her father in the hall below, in earnest conversation. "He is gaining my father's ear about Margery," she thought, "and I can scarce be glad; yet if the child can love him, why, it may be well. I marvel at any woman caring for the mere outside show."

As she thought this, Margery herself came into her sister's room, in a loose white wrapper, girt in at the waist by a black band, and her long hair falling over her shoulders. Margery's face was all lighted with smiles, as she said, "Hyacinth Sacheverell has asked me to be his wife; he loves me, Damaris!"

"Doth he indeed love thee, dear child?" was the answer; and there was a touch of maternal tenderness in her voice, as she drew Margery towards her and kissed her crimson cheek. "Love is ever a beautiful flower, but it needeth to have a deep root, lest it fade and die with the burning heat of this world's troubles and trials."

"Nay, Damaris, you are ever so grave and full of fears, and ifs and buts," Margery exclaimed impatiently. "Can't you wish me joy, for I am right happy. Ah! Damaris, he is so handsome, and hath such gentle ways with him, one must needs give love when he asks for it. Methinks smiles would befit thee better than tears. Why, Damaris!"

Damaris had been much over-wrought that day, and had been trying all through the evening to put a restraint upon herself. Now she utterly gave way, and leaning her head upon her hands, she sobbed bitterly.

"What have I done to grieve thee, Damaris? I love thee, and I have none else to tell of my joy. Be not so doleful, Damaris, while I am so happy."

"Dear child, forgive me," said Damaris, rallying herself. "My life has passed so much amidst the shadows that I cannot, methinks, be as ready as I might to rejoice in the sunshine of others. Dear Margery, if Hyacinth Sacheverell's love is to make thee a happy wife I will rejoice."

" He—Hyacinth—will seek to be a partner in my father's trade, and if he consents, we shall marry forthwith and live here. Thus there will be no breaking up of home, and we shall have merry company, instead of a house as dull as the grave, and Hyacinth saith when the king has his own again, he will take me to court, and that he will get a brocade broidered with pearls which his mother wore, and I can make a brave show with my poor mother's beauteous lace, than which there is none lovelier in the country."

" I would, Margery, you thought less of these ornaments and more of the hidden treasure of the heart; but wisdom may come with years—be that as it may, I wish you God-speed. I must to bed now, for I am weary."

" Where is Grace? I want her to fold my black mantle; and, Damaris, we may be wearing our second mourning soon. I do long to have a little white about me, though Hyacinth saith my hair maketh it beyond possibility that I should be in full mourning; he saith it makes gold settings to my blackness."

"How she doth repeat our poor mother over again," Damaris sighed, as, with another kiss, Margery left her chamber.

"Oh, if she had won a good man's love the future might be brighter for her, but I sorely feel that Master Sacheverell has his own ends in view. A partnership with my father! What will Will Purdy say to that? and is he really trustworthy—this gay, richly attired cavalier, with his fine name and courtly bearing? How different, methinks, from Edward Colston, who would have been as ballast to her little light bark. Ah, me! That I should have pierced that true heart with sorrow—but I am right. I will never wed any man, and far less one who has counted ten years less than myself. Yet, as a dear friend I will ever cherish his memory."

Damaris's musing was interrupted by a tap at the door, and Grace entered. She had conceived an intense love and admiration for Damaris. The visions of the poor Quaker girl had calmed down with quiet, rest, and good food, and though she held firmly to her faith in the moving of the Spirit within, and the guiding of the "inner light," she had, under Damaris's influence, ceased to crave after excitement, and felt that to remain in the house was a more excellent way than to parade the streets.

"I have attended on thy sister," she said. "I have come to crave a few minutes with thee, dear friend and mistress."

"Come hither then, Grace. I am weary and worn with much that I have come through to-day. Open the Testament of our Lord and Saviour and read to me; thy voice soothes me."

"Methinks," said Grace, "I would fain wait on the Lord under covering of silence ere I open the Book. It is that silence which is so blessed a thing during which the still small voice of the Spirit may be heard. But first, dear mistress," Grace said, as she busied herself in putting aside in a deep oak chest Damaris's mantle and gown, smoothing them gently as she did so; "but first I would fain tell thee that our friend Cicely Purdy is much troubled. Her husband is very wroth with something let drop between the master and a gentleman; he has rated poor Cicely as if it were her doing. Verily, she hath the temper of a chosen one of the Lord."

"Aye, indeed. My good Cicely! She hath a thorny path to tread. But, Grace, it seemeth to me that few in these troubled times can expect aught else now," Damaris said, lying back wearily on her bed. "Let us read, for the lamp burns low, and the clocks have chimed for ten."

Grace took a low seat, and, folding her hands, bowed her head, and silence reigned. The oil lamp, placed on a shelf by the wall, shed its radiance over the girl's figure, which was dressed after the fashion of the Puritans of the time. The gown and kerchief provided by Damaris, and the cap made from the pattern, of that which Cicely wore. The scene was one for a poet or painter; that little peaceful spot in the midst of the city where so many hearts were full of bitterness and disappointment; where the upheaval of the late storm which had thrown down the mighty from their seat, was yet felt in the after-shock, of old landmarks swept away, old traditions passed out of sight, old bulwarks of faith and loyalty crumbled into dust. But there, at least, was the faith which no storms could shake; and as Grace opened the Testament and read where she opened, without turning a page or looking to right or left, the words seemed to have a marvellous power as they fell from the lips of the Quaker maiden, whose whole learning was confined to that Book, and reached to nothing beyond it. "Beloved, think it not strange concerning the fiery trial which is to try you, as though some strange thing happened to you: but rejoice, inasmuch, as ye are partakers of Christ's sufferings; that, when His glory shall be revealed, ye may be glad also with exceeding joy. If ye be reproached for the name of Christ, happy are ye; for the spirit of glory and of God resteth upon you: on their part He is evil spoken of, but on your part He is glorified."

Grace paused, and looking at Damaris saw that her eyes were closed; but she read on in her low, sweet monotone to the end of the chapter, and then rising, threw a coverlid over her mistress and gently withdrew.

"The peace that I have craved for is fallen on her," she said softly. "I will serve her till death parts us."

Arrangements were rapidly carried on between Thomas Standfast and Master Hyacinth Sacheverell, and Will Purdy had to accept the proposal of a new head in the merchant's house; with an ill grace, it is true, but there was no alternative.

Margery and Hyacinth were betrothed, and waited only the expiration of the year of mourning to be married.

Thomas Standfast was doubtful as to the wisdom of the plan; but he was an old man, and had been worn out, as many of his fellow-citizens had been, by the troubles he had seen passing around him, and he was glad to be relieved of much of the details of business.

"For Hyacinth has much wit," Thomas Standfast said, as he was talking over the whole matter with Damaris, "and he has good trading connections; and the messenger I sent for his father's consent and certifying of the matter, brings me good news of the stability of the house of Sacheverell in the northern parts. I confess, I would fain this marriage had been with Edward Colston, it would have been on a firmer basis; but there is no rule in matters of love, or I would have said that my Margery's beauty and winning graces might have suited with Edward Colston's sober, quiet demeanour. An alliance with that house would have been a great joy."

Damaris was silent for a moment and then said:

"Hath Edward Colston been to say farewell, father?"

"Nay, and I marvel much thereat. It cannot be, Damaris, that his heart is sore because Margery prefers another to him."

"Nay, I do not think you need fear that, dear father," Damaris said; "but I also marvel that he has not said farewell."

That evening, when Damaris was alone, seated before her table in the bay window, the window where we first saw her as a child, peeping out into the shadows of the street—steps in the room behind her made her start.

"I have come to say my last farewell, Damaris. I sail from the port this night at eleven of the clock. Partings are sore, and it seems to me that I am going away to return no more, or not for many a year, to my native city."

"Have you seen my father?" Damaris asked.

"Yes; I have bid all my farewells. I have

left yours till the last. Damaris, through these ten days I have not dared to approach you, now you will not visit me with your displeasure."

"Nay, Edward, do not speak thus; there is no displeasure in my heart, nought but affection for you, and all love but that love which it is not mine to give to any man."

"I accept all you say, Damaris. I have not the power to tell out the pain which your sweet words gave me ten days agone. I came but to say farewell, and to pray you to hold me in your memory, as I pray God to have you in His holy keeping."

Then as she held out her hand he took it in his once more, and bowing his head over it, whispered, "Wish me God-speed, Damaris."

"May God bless you, Edward Colston," fell on his ear from the lips of the only woman he ever loved, "and make you a blessing."

Then, before she could realise the truth, Edward had kissed the hand he held, and passed out of her sight in the dim shadows of the old oak chamber.

The ship, bound for Spain, loosed from her moorings just as the city churches struck eleven from their belfry towers. She went out with the ebbing tide to the channel's mouth, past the city wharves, past the dark sombre masses of the Leigh woods, past the gigantic forms of the St. Vincent Rocks, which stood revealed, ghost-like, in the light of a moon high in the heavens, which looked out every now and then from behind heavy masses of clouds, driven on the breath of a keen north wind.

Edward Colston, wrapped in his long cloak and with his wide hat well pulled over his brow, stood alone on the deck with many thoughts surging within him, of which his fellow-passengers little dreamed. His father he felt he could scarcely dare to hope he should ever see again, age and infirmity were closing around him. His mother, brave hearted as she was, had seemed to him less able to bear the burden of life, than when he had first returned to Bristol, four months before. His young brothers, who were to follow him, how would they bear themselves on the battle-field of life under new conditions in a foreign country? His little sister Mall would be a woman before he saw her again. Will, little Will, a stripling. All things would be changed; death might come, and the whole aspect of the country be convulsed by yet another revolution, as many wise people deemed must be the case before the heir to the throne came into possession of his own. Yet more bloodshed and strife, and intrigue; yet more persecution in the name of religion; yet more lifting up of the brother's hand against the brother. And amidst all these conflicting thoughts, there came to Edward Colston's mind the words Damaris added to the blessing he had asked for, "and *make you a blessing.*"

It was like a message from heaven; it was, even though he knew it not, a prayer to be richly answered. For he, who was leaving home and country for long years, was to return to fulfil that desire, uttered from the depths of a noble woman's heart, and *be a blessing.*

BOOK III.

A WOMAN'S MESSAGE.

There is a vision in the heart of each,
Of justice, mercy, wisdom, tenderness
To wrong and pain, and knowledge of its cure ;
And these embodied in a woman's form,
The best transmits them, pure as first received
From God above her, to mankind below.
Robert Browning

BOOK III.

1681.

A WOMAN'S MESSAGE.

The June sunshine is once more lying upon the roofs and towers of the old city of Bristol. Twenty-five years have passed since Edward Colston sailed out of the port in a ship bound for Barcelona. A quarter of a century which had brought with it many changes and chances to the people of England.

Time had laid its hand gently on the two women who were seated together in a low hall of Dame Pugsley's mansion, on the crest of Nugent Hill.

A pile of clothes lay before them, and they were sorting them into bundles, as this was the day when the prison doors were opened for many who had been lying in the dismal dungeons of Newgate, and, on their release, needed a friendly hand.

The lady, Joan Pugsley, and her friend,

Mistress Damaris Standfast, were ever ready to help those who were in need, and many a poor prisoner who had been lying in the dark and uncleanly prison cell, would have gone forth only to perish, had not these two brave and loyal-hearted women come to their rescue.

Since the death of Thomas Standfast, Damaris had made her home with her friend, and, united in love and good works, their influence was felt far and wide. The Lady Pugsley had a large household, and a resident chaplain, and all things were done in the greatest order and regularity. Sisters of Charity indeed were these, though bound by no vows, and joined only in the bonds of a common love for a common Lord and Maker.

"The days will come," Dame Pugsley was saying, "when the prison houses will be purified. To think of the horrors of that den where poor Grace's mother breathed her last is sickening, and I fear me, those who go in pure of heart, often come forth contaminated and sin-struck in soul, as well as diseased in body."

"Yes, that poor young woman last month—how she rushed from me and escaped me," Damaris exclaimed; "and hid her poor shame-struck face in the dark waters of the Froom. It seemeth to me that the load of guilt groweth heavier on our rulers as the years pass by; and how little we can do."

"Thou doest thy utmost, Damaris," her friend said. "Hast thou heard more of thy sister this week?"

"No," Damaris answered sadly, "no; methought she might have come up hither again. Poor Margery!"

"If the children are in real want thou knowest, Damaris, my purse is thine for help, but—"

"I know, I know," Damaris exclaimed; "but I greatly fear Hyacinth's debts are far, far beyond temporary help."

"Is he—thy brother-in-law—in Bristol, now?"

"I know not; methinks he is still abroad; the old house is most forlorn; and now dear Cicely is gone, and Will Purdy has given up his post, they are worse than ever. I have done my utmost; but I could not, as you know, stay, and give countenance to much extravagance and feasting when I knew that there was no money to pay for what was consumed. Nevertheless, my heart often yearns over Margery, her troubles are manifold; but how can it be otherwise? Hyacinth runs wild courses, and has no fear of God before his eyes. This peaceful asylum I owe to you, dear friend, or where should I be?"

And now the conversation was interrupted by the appearance of Grace Goldsmith, who said that some of the pensioners had come for their money portions, and that a young man from Mary le Port Street craved leave to see Mistress Damaris.

The messenger was no other than Richard Purdy, the boy Dick, who had so openly expressed himself concerning the Fast-day long years before, and had incurred his father's wrath thereby!

Damaris went out into a smaller room, where Dame Pugsley heard many a tale of woe, and found Dick waiting for her.

"There is great trouble in Mary le Port Street, Mistress Damaris," said Dick; "there is scant food, and most things are gone for debt; but worse than that, little Mistress Hyacintha lies sick with some fever. Mistress Sacheverell begs you to come to her comfort."

"Is thy Master there?"

Dick shook his head. "We have heard no tidings of him for a fortnight past. I hold to the sinking ship while the last plank is above water, as I promised my mother I would; but we are in a sore strait."

"Oh, Dick, faithful Dick!" Damaris exclaimed, "thou hast been a true friend and servant. Take word to my sister that I will be with her at noon. I must needs assist Dame Pugsley, with the linen and gowns for the six poor women who are to be let forth from Newgate to-day, and then I will be with her. Say so to her with my loving greeting."

Dick Purdy made a respectful bow, and was departing, when Damaris called to him. "Stay, Dick; hast thou broken thy fast?"

"No, indeed, Mistress; there is but little chance of that yonder."

"Then come with me to the buttery, and eat. There is some fresh junket just in from the dairy, and milk and rolls. Prythee come, Dick."

Richard Purdy followed with alacrity. He was all but starving, for he had given up his breakfast to Mistress Sacheverell, who was worn out with sorrow and care.

When Hyacinth Sacheverell married Margery Standfast, he had, by agreement with Thomas Standfast, become a partner in the large mercantile firm, which had been prosperous for many years, and took up his abode in the old Mary le Port dwelling.

But advancing age made Thomas Standfast less acute and foreseeing than formerly; many transactions were without his knowledge: heavy losses were the consequence; and Will Purdy, angry and jealous of the new head set over him, instead of putting out a hand to help, after furious altercations and hurling of Scripture texts at poor Thomas Standfast's head, left him and departed to London, where report said he had succeeded in a small business of his own, and was the sun of some Puritan community who basked in his light. Cicely was to have followed him with those of the children who were left. But she died in peace, before the uprooting finally came, and was laid in the family vault of the Standfasts in Mary le Port Church.

She had foreseen the troubles which were coming on Margery, and made Dick promise that he would stand by the daughter of his old master and mistress to the end. How faithfully Dick had fulfilled this promise few outsiders knew. As times grew worse, which they did year by year, Dick was the mainstay of the household.

Hyacinth Sacheverell absented himself for weeks and months, and latterly Margery and little Hyacintha, or Cynthia as she was called, and her brother Charles were often at a loss how to live. Damaris had long ago given up her portion of her father's money to her sister. She had converted almost all her valuable things into money to help her, and did all that could be done, except put herself in the way of her brother-in-law's insolence and rude familiarity. A life of self-indulgence and excess had left but little trace of the handsome young cavalier who had taken Margery's heart by storm. She had built her house upon the sand, and great was the ruin of it.

When Damaris had found it was no longer possible to inhabit the same house as Hyacinth, her friend had taken her into her home with joy, and in their peaceful life of good works and almsdeeds, these two noble women were lifted above the wearisome round of gaiety in which after the Restoration, the Royalists had, in Bristol, as in other parts of the kingdom, indulged.

Now the air was full of the Popish plot, which was filling the gaol with prisoners, and turning the tide of persecution against the Papists, and diverting it from the Quakers and Puritans. Although outwardly there was peace, below the surface, great forces were at work, and no thoughtful person felt any security.

Everything was in a transition state: sometimes one was uppermost, and then another. There seemed to be no anchorage anywhere, for a breath of wind might raise an unlooked-for storm, and the vessel drift off on a trackless sea.

"Little Hyacintha is ailing," Damaris said, when she rejoined her friend. "Dick Purdy feareth a fever, and there is no news of my sister's husband." Damaris always called Hyacinth by that name now.

"Poor souls! You must go at once to their help, and take with thee all that may be needful. Hath a physician seen the child?"

"I know not; but I will call one in if I think it needful."

Damaris departed on her errand soon after twelve, going down Steep Street as her nearest way to the city, and reached the old home of her childhood before one o'clock.

The whole aspect of the desolate mansion was one of decay, and there was a deserted air about the wide hall, which was left bare and unprotected.

As Damaris ascended the oak stairs, the dead

STEEP STREET.

past seemed to rise before her, and give her a pain at her heart, which brought the hot tears to her eyes. There was not a sound to be heard in the large deserted corridors; the heavy oak door on the first floor was half open, and a ray of the brilliant sunshine had pierced the gloom and lay upon the couch, where a child was tossing in a feverish sleep. Seated by her side was a jaded, weary-looking woman, carelessly dressed, and yet with remains of great beauty still to be seen in the graceful lines of her figure and the outline of her delicate profile.

When she saw Damaris she rose, and flung herself into her arms.

"What shall I do? Oh! Damaris, pity me; if this angel is taken from me. Why have you deserted me? You are like all the rest; and I am so miserable."

"I did not dream things were come to so sore a pass, Margery," Damaris said quietly. "You know why I cannot come hither when thy husband is at home."

"He is not here now; he may never return again. He fears being seized by creditors. He has made a journey to his father's house to see if he can get supplies; but Purdy says all the trade is diverted from the house, that the last cargo was seized ere it was unloaded, and that all the folk who were employed have gone over to other merchants. We are ruined, and I and my children are starving. That little one is pining for good food, and the fever which is lurking about her, I do verily think, has brought her so low for this reason."

"I will stay now and nurse her, and if it may be, comfort you, Margery," Damaris said, laying aside her long cloak, and opening the basket she had on her arm. As she did so the same sunbeam which had touched the couch where little Cynthia lay, caught the figure of her aunt, and seemed to encircle it with light.

Women like Damaris Standfast are always beautiful. Although she had nearly reached her fifty-fourth birthday, there was no sign of age or decay about her. Her figure was still erect, and lithe in its movement; and though the masses of hair which were turned back from her forehead were grey, the pencilled brow and lustrous eyes beneath them were even lovelier than of old. Lines there were, round the mouth and eyes— those lines which sorrow and sympathy for the sorrow of others must needs trace; but the shining of the soul is often more beautiful in the eventide than in the morning light.

"I am come to tarry here now, dear Margery," Damaris repeated. "And where is little Charles?"

"Gone forth with Purdy. The boy mopes here, with Cynthia sick, and his mother miserable," was the answer.

"Methinks the child must have a physician," Damaris said, stooping down over Cynthia. "She mutters in her sleep, and her lips are very dry," she continued, putting her cool hand on Cynthia's pulse. "I will raise her in my arms and give her a cooling drink I have brought from Dame Pugsley."

Damaris poured out some of the drink from a flask, and raising Cynthia gently, held a cup to her lips. The child roused herself and drank it eagerly, whispering—

"Aunt Damaris," raising her little hot hand to stroke the face bending over her. "Aunt Damaris, I saw such dreadful dragons coming into the room. Don't let them eat me, will you? They make mother cry. See how she is crying."

Damaris soothed the child by gently swaying her body to and fro, and soon the long lashes rested on the crimson cheeks, and little Cynthia fell again into a heavy slumber.

"Go and lie down, dear Margery, in the inner chamber, and I will watch here until Purdy and Charles return."

"I cannot leave her," Margery moaned; "I must stay here by her side. I am deserted by every one now-a-days. I have only my children. Surely God will not bereave me of Cynthia—my lovely Cynthia."

"He does not willingly afflict us: He will overshadow us with love; for the clouds He sends are love."

"Oh! tell me not that," Margery said impatiently. "Why are some folks prosperous, like Mall Hayman, living like a queen in Small Street, and the Colstons made much of, while *we* are in these straits?"

"There must needs be an answer to that question," Damaris said, with a smile. "We only look through a dark glass. *One day* it will be face to face."

"I don't set such a high price on the Colstons," said Margery. "Mistress Sarah Colston has done me no good turn since the old man died; and why did not that piece of perfectness, Edward, come anear us then? They say he liveth like a noble in London, and all his riches goeth to strangers, while he forgets his native city. I never could put up with him—a prim, stiff and starched fellow, so proper and straight-laced."

"Nay, Margery; these are but idle words. I would not hear more of them. Here is some cold pullet and a fine piece of gammon I will get some ready for you, and with a cup of wine you will feel refreshed. Then seek your bed, and rest, while I watch."

Margery did as she was advised, and retired to her bed, while Damaris, who had laid Cynthia upon the couch, busied herself in making the room tidy, and opened another pane in the lattice to let in more air.

Presently quick steps were heard on the stairs, and a boy of nine or ten years old rushed in.

Damaris held up her hand and pointed to the couch where Cynthia lay.

"Hush, Charley! do not wake her; she sleeps more quietly." The boy obeyed, and then advanced on tip-toe to his aunt, and speaking in a low voice—

"I have seen such a brave sight!" he exclaimed. "Let me tell you about it, Aunt Damaris. Dick took me out to see a grand show. As we got near the Tolzey we saw Master Edward Colston pass in there. All the folks were so grand, and Purdy says he never saw a braver show of knights and dames. There were all the city marshals out in their gowns, and the sheriffs and yeomen. I was standing still, looking at a grand gilt coach which belonged to my lord of Beaufort, when one of the grooms gave me a rough push and called 'Stand back!' Methought it might be His Majesty coming; I should have been hustled in the throng had not Purdy lifted me up on some steps just before the Tolzey. And then, as the crowd gave way, there came a wondrous grave-looking man, with a full wig, walking so slow, while all the rest of the folk were hustling and jostling. And every one bowed and took off their hats; and this man bowed in answer, but he did not smile. He looked as solemn as a minister, and he was not gaudy like the rest. He has lent the city some money, I heard a man say close by, and that he is so wealthy he might pave Bristol streets with gold. This man was very good to me, and he said, 'Youngster, wilt like to get into the Chamber?' 'Aye, would I not?' said I. And then the man said to Purdy, 'Follow on when I move.' And so we did, and passed into the Chamber. The man they all made such an ado about had just got up to the table, and they all rose and bowed. And some one near said, 'It's a fine thing to have a pouch full of gold. That's the way to get folks' hearts.' Then another answered, 'Aye, but Master Colston has a good name, which is better than riches. His fathers before him have had that good name in Bristol.' Do you like me to talk about this, Aunt Damaris? you look so grave."

"Yes, dear boy, I like much to hear of the grand doings. I knew Master Colston when I was young; tell me what happened next."

"Why, the Chamberlain handed Master Colston a paper to read, and he read it with his brows knit, and as if he were pondering every word, just as I ponder my tasks. And then some of the grave gentlemen signed the paper, and then they bowed all round, and the big wigs looked as if they might topple over, and then Master Colston walked down the Hall and bowed right and left, but never smiled. And then he went to Sir William Hayman's in Small Street, and then," Charles added with a yawn and a sigh, " Dick said we must come home."

Dick Purdy now appeared, and Damaris

said, "The child is sickening with fever, Richard. Prythee fetch a physician."

"The barber-surgeon lives close by the bridge; he is very cunning, and his wife is skilled with drugs. But, Mistress Damaris, there is scarce a doit in the house to pay her."

"I will provide that," Damaris said. "It is right to summon him at once; and Richard, I have decided to remain here till I know how it goes with the little one. Will you carry the news to Dame Pugsley for me, and bring back this basket, which I have emptied, full again?"

Richard laughed. "Aye, will I not? It makes me hungry to think of it. There's not much meat or drink here."

"I know it, Dick, I know. I must think over what it is best to do. But Dame Pugsley will come to our aid. Hasten, good Richard, for the surgeon, for my heart misgives about this child. She moans so sadly even while she sleeps."

It was about a fortnight after the day when Edward Colston had signed the deed conveying to the city of Bristol the sum of eighteen hundred pounds, for which he was to receive a 'citie Seale,' next sealing day. A large party was gathering round the hospitable board in the Small Street mansion, where the little Mall of olden times now presided as Dame Hayman, the wife of one of the richest of Bristol's merchant princes.

Unlike her elder brother, and sister Ann, she was ever very vivacious and light-hearted, and her cheerful spirit had infected the large party around her. Mistress Sarah Colston sat at her daughter's right hand, and her eldest son next her, while her youngest was opposite, and there were representatives of several of the old Bristol families present.

Mistress Colston was attired in her long widow's veil and weeds, but her face, always full of intelligence, had now the calm and peaceful expression, which seems like a reflection from the eternal peace into which the most beloved of the soul have entered.

No certain tidings had ever reached her of her two boys who had gone out to Spain soon after their elder brother in 1657, but there was every reason to fear that they had fallen victims to the knife of the assassins who were in league with those piratical robbers who had seized the *Society of Bristol* in the year 1657, some of whom had by Edward Colston's energy been brought to justice. However that might be, the uncertainty and grief at their loss had saddened the declining years of William Colston, who had to the last leaned upon his wife for comfort and support under the weight of trials, of which this was the sorest.

It generally happens that in comforting others we get for ourselves the best comfort, and in supporting them we find our own best stay in trouble. It had been so with Sarah Colston; and now she was as unselfish in her grief as in her joys, and her presence was felt to be a chastening though not a gloomy influence over the family gathered round her.

Sir William Hayman was a man full of conversation and humour, and he liked nothing better than to gather round him the magnates of the city, and talk over the affairs of the kingdom, beginning with Bristol of course, and ending with it, as befitted a good citizen!

He rallied Edward Colston on his reception in the Council Chamber a fortnight before, and asked him why he did not come and take up his abode in Bristol.

"I have taken up my abode here for the present," was the answer; "what more do you want?"

"Aye! a deal more man. We want you to

bring a wife with you; for doubtless there is some fair lady in the case in London. A man who sits at the same governing board with such grand folk as the Bishop of London and Sir George Dashwood, must needs have his pick of society."

"Yes, indeed; and I warrant there is a Mistress Dashwood," said Dame Hayman.

"Tut-tut, Mall, your tongue runneth too fast," said her husband, who saw a frown upon his brother-in-law's face. "But, Edward, we need a Christ's Hospital here. Why spend all your charities in London?"

"You have Queen Elizabeth's Charity," Edward Colston said, "and Whitson's."

"Aye, but there is room for more. Verily, until we have cared for the poor and ignorant there is small hope of the people mending their manners; for ignorance is the mother of much sin."

"Ignorance!" exclaimed a worthy merchant, with his mouth full of a finely seasoned pasty, "Ignorance! you'll find if you give the poor folks over much learning, you'll have a brood of vipers at your heels. Teach 'em to be good workmen with hammer and pickaxe, with knife and needle, but let them leave bookish stuff to their betters."

Sir William Hayman laughed, and a sly twinkle might be seen in Edward Colston's eye, for the worthy magistrate had been known to set his mark to a deed in the Council Chamber.

"Well, well, Edward, you know how the care for the children of the poor works in London. Christ's Hospital ought to speak for itself.

"And so it does. There have been many men already on its rolls of whom England may be proud. The ladder of learning once climbed, the size of the world widens."

"The size of the world!" said the worthy merchant; "I know the size and measurements of Bristol, and that's enough for me. I'll take another snack of that pasty, please your honour, Sir William Hayman."

The conversation then passed to politics, and some of the older men went back over the past history of the kingdom, dwelling on many details of personal remembrance, which were interesting as from eye-witnesses.

In a company like this, the name of Charles the First was still mentioned in an almost reverent tone. His faults were all covered by the robe of martyrdom, and indeed well might men ask each other in the year 1682, what had been gained for the nation by the great rebellion?

There was abundant cause for anxiety while Charles the Second lived. The evils of another Revolution might be kept in abeyance, but Charles was confessedly leading a life of excess, which could hardly be a long one, and the storm of terror the Popish plot had raised scarcely four years before, still lingered in the horizon, and boded ill for the peace and safety of the country.

The House of Commons had voted for the exclusion of the Duke of York from the throne, and though the bill was thrown out in the Lords, the large majority in the Commons of seventy-five votes, showed the temper of the times.

Charles had dissolved the Parliament, and called a new one at Oxford, as the excitement in London was too great to render a meeting there safe.

It was a mere farce, and was dissolved without transacting any business, and it was Charles's last Parliament. He was at this time ruling as an absolute monarch, and the hearts of many brave and faithful subjects were heavy within them.

No wonder that men like Edward Colston, who had the strongest allegiance to the Reformed Church, and an equally strong aversion to any departure from its rubrics and liturgy, should, in the midst of much personal and family prosperity, look with foreboding on the future, and with sorrow on the past history of his country.

The Duke of Monmouth was already singled out as the means of upsetting the order of succession, and what further subversion of order lay in the coming years who could tell? The more intelligent of the guests at Sir William Hayman's table were anxious to draw out Edward Colston as to the opinions of the great London world, to which, by virtue of his place on the board of Christ's Hospital, he was supposed to belong, and he was, though reticent on most subjects, eloquent on all matters connected with the Church.

Those were the times of strong religious feeling; very few people who professed to be religious at all, were half-hearted or luke-warm.

The giant force of Cromwell's character had as it were penetrated the mass of the Presbyterian people, and Puritan fervour had by no means died out with the great leader whose soul had departed amidst the roar of the thunder, and the flash of the lightning.

The Quaker spirit was also at this time at the very zenith of fervid zeal. Hunted from place to place, scourged, mocked, and buffeted, the followers of George Fox continued to increase and flourish, and during the latter part of this seventeenth century formed themselves into that body, with its strict organizations and rigid rules, which has stood the storms of two centuries. The Church, as by law established, had also much vitality, and the clergy were jealous of any approach to the doctrines and practices of the men who had for some years been in possession of their livings, preached from their pulpits, and usurped authority in the Church, whence they were driven as outcasts.

Edward Colston was a thorough Conservative, and, perhaps it must be conceded, a bigoted one. But in looking back on those days, it is necessary to keep in mind that amongst the factions and unrest of the times, law-abiding people watched jealously the first sign of an approaching storm, which might again sweep over the face of the country with the besom of destruction.

When the guests were all gone, and silence had fallen on the spacious rooms of the Small Street mansion, Edward Colston sat in one of the upper chambers with his books and writing materials before him. He leaned back wearily in his chair, and after having made a statement of his transaction in the Council Chamber that day, in a large cumbrous book with very thick binding, he laid down the pen and resigned himself to meditation. The past rose before him, peopled with the images of those who were gone. One face seemed to appear with a strange persistence, and Damaris Standfast lived again for him in her beautiful and gracious womanhood, and her voice seemed to sound in his ear, in all its musical rich tones as she spoke of woman's special mission to seek out and to teach the poor and the ignorant.

He had heard of all the fair deeds of charity wrought by her and Dame Pugsley, and he had longed to go up to that house on the Hill, and look once more on Damaris.

The stiffness and reserve of his early days had not relaxed with age, and he had during the short time he had spent in his native city, tried in vain to summon courage to seek out the only woman he had ever loved. The history of the Sacheverell troubles had reached him, and he heard from his mother that it was in vain to try to help Margery; she would squander money on finery, and let the debts pass.

Then Sarah Colston had said—

"She is so puffed up and full of conceits, that it is irksome to go near her, but she hath a nice little maid named after her father, Hyacintha, and I do not love to think of her in need."

"I will seek them out to-morrow," was the end of Edward Colston's meditation, and he was about to prepare to lie down to rest, when the man who had the charge of the night watch in the hall, tapped at the door.

"Who goes there?" he asked.

"There is some one below, your honour, who is in dire distress, and prayed me to summon you."

Edward Colston had opened the door by this time and asked—

"What is his need?"

"Your honour, it is a woman, who has her hood so close drawn over her face I can make out no feature by the light of the lamp."

"It is an unseemly time for a woman to be abroad; is she unattended?"

"I see no one with her in the court, your honour; but I believe she is in great need, she is speaking between her sobs of a child who is sick, and said that did you know of her trouble, you would relieve her."

Edward Colston waved his hand.

"I will follow you," he said, and then he prepared to go downstairs, with the stately, leisurely tread which was so characteristic of his whole character. He never hurried or lost his presence of mind: deliberate in all his deeds of charity, they were the outcome of much thought and consideration.

He approached the closely-veiled figure standing in the large hall, and said, "What brings you forth at near eleven of the clock? Hark!"—as the voice of a band of revellers sounded from the street—"hark! this is no hour for women to be abroad."

"Master Colston, I am Margery Sacheverell. I am in sore need. My husband is in hiding; for he is steeped in debt and dishonour. Fever has come to my poor deserted home, and stricken my Cynthia low. Richard Purdy has sickened to-day, and my poor boy has been saved only by his removal to Dame Pugsley's. I am in want of bread, and I am come hither at the express desire of my sister, Damaris Standfast."

A perceptible change passed over Edward Colston's face. "Your sister!" he exclaimed, "tell her—"

"Alas! alas!" sobbed Margery, "no words of yours can reach her now; she is dead. I would you could look on her face as she lieth in the chamber where she has nursed my child. The fever made great havoc with her. They let blood yesterday, and though the fever abated, she sank off and died as the curfew tolled from St. Nicholas' Tower this evening. She bid me seek you, for she said, 'He promised to succour me or any whom I loved;' and she added, 'Edward Colston can never change.'"

Margery was almost frightened at the stern hard voice which repeated her words, "Edward Colston can never change," and then, without another word, he turned away and went upstairs.

His own servant slept in a small chamber next his own, and he called him.

"Take a flask of wine, and all that you can find of nourishment from the buttery, and make all haste; then attend Mistress Sacheverell to her house in Mary le Port Street, and say I will be with her anon. Do as I bid you," he said sternly, as the servant, sleepy and greatly wondering, prepared to obey. "Speed, yes," he said, "make all speed; but for her—for her it is too late."

Then Edward Colston disappeared within his chamber and bolted the door.

The servant, by no means pleased to be disturbed, did his bidding, and delivered the message to Margery Sacheverell. There was no need to light the torch, for a full moon high in the heavens bathed the city in a soft and tender radiance, casting the dark shadows of the high gables on the streets, and making the gilt cross shine out like a star.

But the moon had set and the summer sun had arisen to bless the earth once more ere Edward Colston left his room and again descended the wide hall-stairs.

The night watcher was asleep on his bench, his own servant, having performed his mission, had stretched himself out on another settle by the empty hearth, and no eyes were upon the grave stern man who stepped out of the courtyard into the street, with a face on which the traces of a long struggle were plainly traced. No one can tell what that struggle had been; but it was over now, and calmly and deliberately Edward Colston crossed over to the corner of Mary le Port Street, and passed into the shadows of the overhanging bays and pointed roofs of the stately mansions most of which have long since disappeared.

He found Margery Sacheverell sleeping the sleep of sorrow and exhaustion in the large room which has been so often described. A little fair-haired girl was at her side, with a wan, thin face and sunken cheeks, on which the fringed eyelashes lay motionless.

Cynthia had passed the crisis of her illness, but was now only the shadow of her former self. Everything was still—still with the silence of death. The door into the next chamber was open, and Edward Colston knew, as if by inspiration, that all that was left of Damaris Standfast lay there.

He advanced slowly, his hands clasped tightly together, his lips set, his whole bearing that of repressed emotion—emotion repressed with a determination that was absolute pain. A pale sorrow-stricken woman in Quaker garb rose, when Edward Colston stood in the doorway, but she did not speak.

Grace Goldsmith had been holding spiritual communion by the dead, and her pale face had an ethereal and wrapt expression on it, as if she had followed the spirit of her mistress and friend into the unseen world, and had been called by Edward Colston's entrance back to this

She spoke no word, but retired from her position by the bed, and Edward Colston drew near and gazed at the still face he had loved so well.

The pure light of the morning came through the high windows, and fell upon the beautiful countenance of Damaris Standfast. The lines which time and care had traced on that noble brow were all smoothed out now. There was no sign of pain, or age, or sorrow left. Dame Pugsley had crossed the long, slender hands upon the quiet breast, and had allowed no one but herself to touch the form of her who had been one with her in her sorrow and her deeds of ministering love. She had retired to sleep and take needful rest, leaving Grace to watch.

As Edward Colston gazed upon that calm face, his heart seemed to soften within him. The deep well of his old love sprang up and sent the gentle rain of tears from his eyes.

"Beloved!" he said in a low whisper, "I cannot change; thou hast judged me aright. I will perform my promise to thee, Damaris, and thy sister shall be cared for; the poor shall be cared for here in thy native city; the ignorant shall be taught, and henceforth I will make the widow my wife, and the fatherless my children."

Then from out the far past came to his soul

a message of hope, and of consolation—from the window in the old chapel, which had long since been demolished. The sweet face, with its saintly, stedfast gaze, was before him in its likeness to that other face now wrapt in the beauty of the sleep that knows no waking, and he murmured as he stooped down and kissed the calm, untroubled brow:

"I shall meet thee again; for, beloved, *expecto vitam venturi sæculi.*"

When Margery Sacheverell awoke from her sleep, roused by her child's little wailing cry for Aunt Damaris, she found lying upon a table near her a sealed packet. She roused herself to open it, and on a slip of paper she read:—

"For the sustenance and consolation of the sister she loved—in fulfilment of my promise.
"E. C."

The packet contained drafts and bills for several thousand pounds.

As Edward Colston passed out of the hall, he met the husband and father coming in.

"My child, doth she live?" he asked. "I am hunted down by the birds of prey, but I could not rest till I heard tidings of little Cynthia."

"She lives, and will do well; you are a free man now, for relief has come for your necessities."

Hyacinth stared like a man in a dream at Edward Colston, and staggered upstairs to find his wife and child.

BOOK IV.

THE END OF THE JOURNEY.

"Rest comes at length, though life be long and dreary,
  The day must dawn, and darksome night be past,
Faith's journey ends in welcomes to the weary,
  And heaven, the heart's true home, will come at last.

"And with the morn those angel faces smile,
  Which we have loved long since, and lost awhile."

BOOK IV.

THE END OF THE JOURNEY.
1710.

THE March sunshine was welcome after a long spell of wintry weather. In the sheltered nooks of a wide-spreading garden it was quite warm, and the primroses were showing little pale yellow buds amongst the large crinkled leaves, while here and there, a full-blown flower smiled out its welcome to the spring.

Along a straight gravel path a child was walking demurely; such a small delicate child, that she scarcely looked her age of seven years. Her face was almost hidden by the warm hood which was tied closely under her chin, but a pair of wistful eyes with a far-away earnest gaze, were turned up to the branches of a wide-spreading cedar to the left of the path, where a bird was answering the smile of the little primrose at its root, by a song, and the burden of the song was "Spring is coming."

The child did not pause long, but walked on till she came to a wide expanse of close shaven turf, in the centre of which was a quaint octagonal summer-house, surmounted by a pedestal and gilt ball, which was shining like a mimic sun in the golden noonday light. The summer-house had a tiled floor in black and white chequer work, and was perfectly dry and air-tight. Eight little windows admitted the light, and a rustic table stood in the middle of the floor, as the summer-house stood in the middle of the greensward.

This summer-house was a favourite resort of the little lonely girl, who had no playfellows or young companions, but only the society of a great-uncle and great-aunt, who had taken care of her during the greater part of her little life, and stood in the place of father and mother to her. Little Say was a precocious child, and was already able to read out of the large printed Testament to her uncle, with precision and fluency, and perform feats of tapestry stitch as she sat on a low stool by her aunt's side in the dim quiet blue drawing-room, scented with dried lavender and rose-leaves, where sounds from the busy world of the great city a few miles distant could not penetrate.

Say, or Sarah Colston, knew nothing of that

city, or of any city, by actual experience, but she was full of curiosity about it, and now as she climbed on the seat which ran round the summerhouse, she put her small face close to one of the eight windows, from which she could see a bend of the river, up which the pleasure barges from London came with bands of music on summer days.

Say speculated much about that city, and another in the far west, where every now and then she knew her uncle, Edward Colston, went in the great chariot drawn by four horses, and where her aunt Nan told her he had fed and clothed the orphans, and provided a hospital for the old and infirm, on the brow of St. Michael's Hill. Indeed, little Say knew much of her uncle's good deeds in Bristol by heart though her aunt would often wind up her information on a subject dear to them both by adding—

"These are the deeds thy uncle hath wrought in the sight of all men, but he hath many more recorded on high, which are seen only by the Father who seeth in secret."

Mistress Ann Colston had great powers of description, and inherited a certain grace of manner, and at times a sprightliness from her mother, Sarah Colston.

Little Say's meditations were now broken in upon by the tap of her aunt's stick upon the gravel path at some distance; but the child caught the sound, and slipping down from her perch, ran across the turf, to meet a tall old lady, whose form was still erect for her age, and whose voice was pleasant and cheery.

"Ah, little one, so thou didst run off before I could catch thee. Fie, then, not to wait for thy old aunt."

"I wanted to get to the summer-house to see if any barges were coming up the river. I would my uncle would take me to London with him some day."

"He will do so some day. The country air is best for little maids, and there are but few roses ever blushing on thy pale cheeks;"— and Mrs. Ann Colston tapped Say's cheek with the knob of her silver-headed cane.

"I would like to see the town, and the folks there; the Queen, and the gilt coach and barge," the child said; "and I would vastly like to see the large house, and all the little girls and boys at Bristol. Next time Uncle Edward sets off in the big coach, I will tell him to take me with him."

"A likely matter, indeed, that a child of tender years should go through the long and toilsome journey to Bristol."

"I was younger when I was brought hither," said little Say, with ready quickness. "I was but twelvemonths and a day, so Pepita has told me often. If I could bear the journey here then, it would not hurt me now. I should so dearly like to see the house where you were a little maid, Aunt Nan, and where grandmother lived, and the blessed King Charles, who was murdered by wicked men, abode."

"Dear heart!" exclaimed Mistress Ann Colston, "to hear the child talk! A babe in years, but a woman grown in wisdom."

"Nay, I will not sit down," she said, as little Say climbed once more upon the bench of the summer-house, and motioned to her aunt to sit beside her. "The March wind is keen, and finds its way to old bones through the chinks of the summer-house. We will take a turn towards the river. It may be thy uncle's barge is now returning."

Say descended once more from her elevation, and tripped by her aunt's side along a path sheltered by a thick cypress hedge on one side and lofty trees on the other, which led them to the bank of the Thames. Here the warmth of the noonday sun triumphed over the sharpness of the March wind, and the little wavelets of the swift-flowing river were sparkling like diamonds as they danced amongst the rushes at the foot of the high bank.

Say was never allowed to go near the river alone, and even now her aunt caught her hand, and said, "Keep near me, child, and do not walk too close to the water's edge. We will take one turn, and then retrace our steps towards the house by the green path."

Little Say walked quietly by the old lady's side, and was silent for a few minutes. Presently she said:

"Pepita saith Uncle Edward is soon to open the great house at Bristol for all the children to whom he gives food and clothing. I shall beg him to take me with him."

"Aye, beg as you will, child, your uncle will not grant that prayer. Dost thou not know that the journey is long, and the roads not too safe by reason of the highwaymen and discontented folk who lurk in the wilds of Putney Heath, and can by no means be kept in check? Why, only last evening Master Jones was telling of a gentleman whose coach was surrounded in a twinkling, and he was rifled of every coin he possessed—aye, and frightened to boot, so that he has fallen into fits ever since."

"Uncle Edward has never been yet waylaid," said the child. "God takes care of him who taketh care of the poor and needy."

"What a child it is!" exclaimed the old lady again, half to herself and half aloud. "But she needeth playmates, and is getting too wise for her tender years. Pepita is right."

Pepita was the little girl's pet name for the housekeeper, who was in truth the real mistress of Edward Colston's establishment at Mortlake, and ruled there with a potent sway, restraining, as she thought, some of her master's superfluous charities.

She was always ready to point out the sins and shortcomings of those who were continually relieved from the kitchen department at Mortlake, where supplies of broth and soup were dispensed by the master's order.

But year by year she found that the bounty grew rather than diminished, and that she could not stem the current of that noble stream of charity which was flowing onwards with ever-widening borders to be lost in the ocean of eternal love.

As little Say and her aunt turned at the end of the broad walk by the river the child exclaimed—

"Aye! there is the barge! and there are my uncle and Master Jones stepping out. Prythee let me run to greet them!"

"Nay, child, be careful; a false step and—" But Say was gone. Her little face was flushed with the tenderest pink as she flew towards the stately form which was advancing from the steps of the boat-house.

All that dignity and stately grace which had given an idea of stiffness and reserve in younger days, now added a charm to the tall figure of the old man, who carried his head erect in spite of the weight of seventy-five years, and walked with firm if slow step, along the terrace path, his friend, in the recognized clerical dress of the time, by his side—shovel hat, knee breeches, and tightly fitting long coat of best broadcloth, with long plain cambric neck-tie, and cuffs. Edward Colston smiled upon little Sarah with that rare sweet smile which his sister said was kept for her alone.

"The wind is in the east though the sun is hot. Have a care, little one, that thy hood is fastened close," he said, bending down with tender solicitude to the child.

"I have a great thing to ask of thee, Uncle, prythee."

"Thy manners, Say; pay thy respects to Master Jones."

"Nay, nay, I never catch a smile or a word when you are by," said the good clergyman, whose broad, rosy face was always good-tempered and benign in its expression. "I'll take a kiss as a penance," and Master Jones bent down to carry out his threat when Say drew back.

"I wish you good-day, your reverence," and then with a deep curtesy she retreated to the shelter of her uncle's side.

Master Jones laughed loudly, and the servants who were carrying cloaks and furs from the barge looked at each other and smiled, the foremost of them, a negro, showing his white teeth from ear to ear.

Mistress Ann Colston now came up, and the four turned towards the house from the river, little Say clinging to her uncle's hand, while Master Jones kept near Mistress Ann Colston.

"When you next go to Bristol, Uncle Edward, prythee take me. Pepita saith it will be a grand sight when the great house is opened for the children. Say yes!"

"A great deal hangs on that *yes*, little sprite.

I must consider it well. Thou knowest I always look well before I leap."

The child pressed the hand which held hers fast, and said, "I know—" and then added, "Why had you never a little child of your very own?"

"Those children at Bristol are as my very own; and what are you, but close to your old uncle's heart? What child could be closer?"

Another assuring pressure of the hand she held, and then crossing the lawn they reached the entrance of the house, and here Master Jones took leave of his friends, saying he must return to dine with his wife, who would be wearying to see him.

"She watches for my coming," he said, "from the little side window in the parsonage, and I never disappoint her now age is coming over her."

"That is well said," Edward Colston remarked with a sigh; "happy are you, Master Jones, to have a wife who looks for your coming with eager anticipation, and mourns for your absence. Present my respectful duty to Mistress Jones; and so good-day, with thanks for your company in London."

Edward Colston turned to the library, and

his sister to her chamber, while little Sarah went to hold some conversation with Pepita, who was superintending the preparation for the supper, and who always welcomed the little maiden with a smile and some dainty she had put aside for her. Say liked these visits to Pepita, and to-day she was well pleased when the housekeeper removed her hood and cloak, and drawing a large carved oak chair to a bright fire sat down in it and took the child on her knee.

"Here is some conserve of ginger and thin biscuits. Eat them, sweetheart, and taste the cordial, for you are as cold as charity."

"I am not cold, Pepita, but it is comforting to feel the heat, and I daresay I am tired a bit. Tell me some nice story to while away the time," Say said, as she nibbled her wafer and took tiny bits of ginger from the point of a silver knife which Pepita held to her mouth.

"I wish I could find a child to play with you," said Pepita with a sigh. "That is what you want more than stories."

"No," said little Say, "I don't; I like to hear your stories over and over again. Do tell me why Uncle Edward never had any little children of his own."

"Ah!" said Pepita, responding to the question, as Say knew she would, for she had often asked it before.

"Ah! that's more than any can tell! so rich and good a gentleman might have married any lady in the land. But I have heard the Bristol folks say—when one or other has chanced to come hither—that he never goes to the city but he visits the grave of the good lady, Dame Pugsley, and that she knew about him more than anyone, and that there was a beautiful lady, her friend, whom the master loved."

"But, dear heart!" Pepita exclaimed, "to talk like this to a baby like you!"

"I like it," said the child. "Pepita, who was the beautiful lady?"

"That's more than I know. She died of a fever caught—so they say—by nursing other folk. A fever raged in Bristol, in the reign of the second King Charles, who came to the throne after that great rebel Cromwell died."

"Oh! Pepita, is it true *he* lived here? I wish it was not true. I am so afraid of the dark place where they say he hid for fear of some folks coming to kill him, as he had killed the king, the blessed king."

"Well, well, think no more on't now, it's not for little maids to trouble their heads about it. We will talk about the poor debtors the master has set free to-day. For James says that he and Master Jones went straight to the Marshalsea, and that it was enough to melt a heart of stone, to see the poor creatures as they were freed of their debts, falling down and kissing the very ground the master walked on. And then Master Jones spoke up so beautiful of the Lord, who has paid our debts and set us free. Well-a-day! the master gets often taken in shameful, and that is enow to anger a saint. Only yesterday a man comes up limping and sighing and groaning. And, says he, he could scarce cross the common for dreadful pain in his leg, and that it was St. Anthony's fire burning in it. The master had watched him as he came out of church, and he got a deal more, I warrant, than the pipkin of broth. And he whined and cried, and said the master was an angel. When this very morning I was in the village and I saw the rogue shouldering a pickaxe, and off to work as merry as a cricket. I gave him a bit of my mind, and he looked as sheepish a fool as I ever saw."

Pepita's voice had a soothing effect on little

Say. When she started on a string of anecdotes, one led on to another, and the end was far off. Pepita never required any remark or comment on her narrative; indeed, she rather preferred silence. So as little Say's head sank gently on her broad breast, and the white eyelids with their delicate blue veins, closed over her violet eyes, the good woman talked on, telling stories of her master's goodness to the workmen in Bristol, of his turning the grindstone when the workman was absent, and buying a brand new hat for a labourer who was engaged in building the hospital.

At last Pepita's domestic duties asserted themselves in the shape of a request from the cook, that she would come and mix the herbs for the hot drink, with which Edward Colston always finished his meal. She rose therefore with the sleeping child in her arms, and carried her into the blue drawing-room where Mistress Ann Colston was sitting with her spinning-wheel.

"I'll just lay her down, dear lamb, on this settle," Pepita said; "it is a pity to arouse her."

"Yes, sweet lamb," the old aunt said, bending over Say. "Methinks, Pepita, it might be good for her to go with her uncle to Bristol.

She is too quiet and thoughtful for her tender years. A playmate is what she needs. The child lives amidst us old folks, and though she is the light of this house, still age shadows youth, and it is not altogether right to suffer it."

When little Say was in bed that night, the two old people sat together in the blue drawing-room. The March evening was chill, and the merry blaze from the logs on the hearth was cheerful. The light fell upon the portraits of the father and mother, now both passed to their rest, and the only two of their children yet left on earth were Ann and Edward Colston. They had lived to see many many changes in the realm. The fall and rising again of the Stuart dynasty, the great reaction which followed the return of Charles the Second, when the long pent-up stream of pleasure and revelry burst forth in a flood which threatened to destroy the landmarks of morality, and all social bonds. The two great parties in the religious world had broken up into many various shades of opinion. Each one held his own with a tenacity which savoured of bigotry, and the Church as by law established was in perpetual antagonism with those who set it at defiance, casting off the dust from their feet, and proclaiming themselves free of her shackles.

Through all changes and through all chances, Edward Colston had remained stedfast to the old faith, and if his loyalty to the Church made him at times censorious and hard, it must be remembered how much he had seen of suffering, of rebuke and shame, when his father had escaped barely with his life from the persecution of the Puritan faction which so long held its own in his native city. There is no doubt that the time-serving and wily cant of the Corporation of that ancient city of the west; the preaching which was often but feebly brought into practice; the "seeming to be religious," which was too often but seeming; had tended to strengthen Edward Colston into an unbending allegiance to every form and every tradition of the Church of England.

It was the very nature of this man to see before him the straight line of what he conceived to be the path of duty, and to be impatient and intolerant of those who might differ from him, and venture to suggest that the Puritan and the Quaker, the Baptist and the Independent might perchance see the true light which lighteth every man, though with a vision obscured, very often by vain conceits and the self-exaltation, which they mistook for self-abasement.

"There is yet great talk in the town, sister, concerning Dr. Sacheverell; the folks are making much ado about the burning of his sermons, and I hear her Majesty is full of indignation against the persecutors."

"Aye, and well she may be," said Mistress Ann Colston; "but the clamour will only strengthen the hands of the Church, and all good and loyal people will see that our safety lies in holding fast to her."

"Yes! that is well spoken," Edward Colston said; "but these are stormy times full of rancour. Indeed, looking back on my long life, what mischief have I not seen hatched in the name of religious zeal?"

"They do say the ministry is hastening to its fall, and if the Church party and law-abiding folk get the helm, there may be more hope for the kingdom. Ever since there has been such talk of Dr. Sacheverell, brother, I have ransacked my brain as to where I had heard the name, and to-day it came to me. The gay worthless husband of Margery Standfast was Hyacinth Sacheverell."

"Yes," Edward Colston replied. "Did you not know that he came of the same stock, though not nearly related. Merchants in the north country, from which sprang many branches, and this reverend and worthy doctor was one of them."

"Are any of Margery's children or grand-children living?"

"Had you asked me that question, sister, yesterday, I could not have answered it; but this very day I had knowledge of the existence of a grandson of hers, the son of Cynthia, who married, as you know, a son of one of the Aldworths."

"Ah, yes, but my memory will not serve me as yours does, brother; still I have a dreamy notion that once in the time of a terrible fever Damaris Standfast—"

Edward Colston finished the sentence, almost hastily interrupting his sister.

"Nursed her, and tended her, and died in the fever. It chimes eight. I go to my library, sister, and will wish you good-night."

"Yes, it is time to retire, methinks; but surely you are over-tired, Edward: these days in London are ever too much burden for you."

"We grow old apace, sister, but methinks

these river journeys in the easy floating barge are rather a rest than a toil. The child—our fair flower—looked very fragile to-day; beware of these east winds, which are wont to nip many tender buds."

"How his heart is set on that child!" Mistress Ann thought, as her brother left the room to seek the retirement of his library.

Here a lamp was lighted, and his black servant waited on him with a cup of hot wine well spiced, and some delicate ginger cakes, like those with which Pepita had fed little Say, when she came in from her walk by the river.

Edward Colston seated himself by his table covered with papers, and dismissing the boy, who made him a respectful reverence at the door, he fell into deep musing. A chord had been touched in his heart that day. The very name of the man who had been the chief subject of town and country talk for the last few weeks, had been as the hand of the magician to call back the past.

All through that protracted trial in the House of Lords, when Dr. Sacheverell had been arraigned before the Peers, and the Queen had been a listener to the angry denunciations by the Bishops, and the defence set up for the learned doctor, there had been in Edward Colston's heart a memory of the name of the accused man that was bound up with his very life. He had known that Margery and her husband, with their son and daughter, had left Bristol, and by the help of his money had sailed for America, and he had heard but little more. And now this very day he had been accosted by a young man who introduced himself as a grandson of Master Hyacinth Sacheverell, who had married a Bristol lady, one Margery Standfast. He had found him waiting at the door of Christ's Hospital hall, where, after his visit to the Marshalsea, he had called for letters. The young man had come over from America with an earnest desire to pursue his studies at one of the English universities, and showed Edward Colston a letter signed by his mother, Cynthia Aldworth, late Cynthia Sacheverell.

Edward Colston had responded, the boy thought, somewhat stiffly, giving the long letter a cursory glance, and merely bidding him to Mortlake on any day that suited his convenience. The young man had turned away, disappointed, saying—" Any day is no day;" but one of the gentlemen in the hall, noticing his disappointed look, said:

"You must not, young sir, judge the intentions or the character of Master Colston by first impressions. He may have a cold manner; but there never beat a nobler and warmer heart in any man."

"I think I choose rather a warmer manner," said the youth. "That old gentleman has got all the air of your proud Tory folk."

"Hush now," said the gentleman, "that is a rash speech for a stranger. Party spirit is at high-water mark now. And I give you two bits of counsel; keep your opinions to yourself, and go the first day possible to Mortlake, where, if I mistake not, all who want a friend find one."

The young man shrugged his shoulders, and settling his broad lace cravat and heavy curled locks, he walked away.

Although Edward Colston had responded but coldly to the young man, now he was alone he drew out of a deep leather pouch the letter which he had presented to him and scanned it with attention.

It was addressed from Pennsylvania, and when read more carefully, there could be little doubt of its authenticity.

The writing was clear and legible, and told of good education.

It ran thus:—

"Dear and honoured sir,

"I address you with some sinkings of heart, and pray that you will not spurn me from your feet. The favour I beg is that you will give the support of your countenance to my young son, Hyacinth Aldworth, who may claim kindness and benevolence at your hands on the score of birth. I, his too unhappy mother, am the widow of Roger Aldworth, a nephew of the Bristol merchant of that name. So far, methinks, he has a claim of citizenship on your goodness; but further, I am the only surviving child of one Margery Sacheverell. From my mother, aye, and from my father also—both as I pray and believe, entered into rest—I have heard of your benevolence to them in sore need. My mother recalled well how you saved her in direst distress, and that by your munificence she and her husband, my poor father, were enabled to set sail for America.

"But small prosperity followed them thither. My father's health broke, and my poor mother could scarce keep us, till at length my husband was sent to be our good angel, and by his labour of love restored us to some measure of prosperity.

"I have but this only son. God has taken from me all my other children. My eldest born was named Damaris, in memory of my mother's dearly-loved sister, who died of a cruel fever when I was a little child. I ask your kindness for my son; he has upon him a restless craving for study, as he thinks. For my part, I mourn that he should leave his widowed mother. He would fain that I crossed the ocean with him; but my heart failed me; and yet I shall go through agonies of fear when I think of him making that long perilous voyage. He saith that when he has studied law at Oxford, or in the Temple in London, he will return for me, and bring me to his home in the old country. But, ah! I fear me I shall never see his face again. I pray God to keep him in morality and purity of life. And oh! dear sir, I pray you to extend to him a kindly hand out of the benevolence of your large heart.

"I am your humble servant, with respect,
"Hyacintha Aldworth,
"(late) Hyacintha Sacheverell."

"I would I had read this letter more carefully," Edward Colston thought, "I hurriedly scanned it. Well, I must find out the youth, launched on the perilous tide of London life, far more perilous than the ocean of which his mother writes. The name, the name herein," he went on, folding the letter slowly in its proper creases. "That name, how it is as a key to open the doors of the past; and I see before me noble, beautiful Damaris. I am an old man, to whom the world points as successful and prosperous; aye, and it praises me for my deeds of charity and for my care of the young, and for my zeal in having them taught. None know that whatever I do for the little ones comes from *her;* from her I first learned the blessedness of service, from her, who, though never mine, is yet always mine; near me in spirit even now—Damaris!" He pronounced her name aloud, and closing his eyes, there rose before him the window, the little window in the old chapel. The face looking from it with its unearthly beauty, and the words were slowly uttered—

"I believe, yes, thank God, I believe in the life of the world to come."

Then after a moment's pause, he seemed to throw aside the past, and to live in the present once more.

He took a pen and wrote on a slip of paper:

"Mem.—that I find out the whereabouts of the young man, Hyacinth Aldworth," and then he became engrossed with the detail of the dress of his boys, who were so soon to gather in the Great House in St. Augustine's Back, and went over carefully and precisely all the articles he deemed necessary for them.

Nothing was neglected in his methodical mind. Suit of clothes, cap, band, shirt, stockings, shoes, buckles, spoon and porringer, all stood with the value jotted down against them, and the cash reckoned for the cost of each boy. Then there were final arrangements to make respecting brewing utensils and barrels, and bedding, sheets, and towels, and nothing of this kind was done by deputy. Edward Colston spared no trouble about anything he undertook. He was not one of those rich people who give a sum of money to some charitable object, and then forget all about it, and care nothing as to how it is administered. He certainly carried out to the letter the instructions of the catechism, which he took every pains should be taught to the children, and "was true and just in all his dealings." Too true and just for some of the Bristol magnates, who were chafed, as we may remember, in times past, by his insisting on the payment of a debt from the Council, which he said he never intended to be a gift.

The Temple School was one of the charities in which he took an especial interest, and the clergyman of the Temple Church, Master Arthur Bedford, was one of his best friends, and the labours of the day were closed by a letter he wrote to him, expressing his satisfaction in the letter he had received from Sir John Duddlestone praising the excellent training of the forty-four poor boys in the Temple School.

At last all was finished, and putting away his writing materials, he opened the large Prayer Book which rested on a carved oak stand, and read the Psalms for the 24th evening, and then the old man bowed his head and prayed.

The March wind sighed in the leafless branches of the noble trees, and a crescent moon was sinking below the meadows which stretched out beyond the river. An atmosphere of peace seemed to surround the house, as its master walked slowly to his room with a small lamp in his hand.

The servants were all in their beds, for the clock had struck twelve, and the slow deliberate steps as Edward Colston ascended the stairs, was the only sound. On the first landing he paused by a half-open door, and a child's voice was heard.

"Uncle Edward! I am so wakeful. Come in."

The old man went into the little room, which was a sort of glass closet or ante-room to that occupied by Mistress Ann Colston. He shaded the lamp he held carefully, and looked down at the child with a long gaze.

"Nay, Sarah, my little maid, you ought to be sleeping."

"I could not sleep. I do so want to go to Bristol next time you go thither, to see the place where my grandfather lived, and the great house where your little boys and girls are to live. Do, I pray you, uncle, say you will take me. Promise, for when you promise you never, never change."

The sweet pleading face, and the little child-like treble voice rising and falling in her eagerness, was not to be resisted.

"Yes, yes, dear child, I promise, and so now be content."

"Oh! I am content," she said. "I wish you good-night, good-night," and then little Say turned upon her pillow, and with her uncle's blessing fervently uttered, she was soon asleep.

The vicar of the Temple Church, the Rev.

Arthur Bedford, was a man who never insisted on the dignity of his office, as some of the clergy thought their duty in those times, when, as we know, not so many years before, the beneficed clergy were turned adrift, and the pulpits filled by untrained and often fanatical preachers of no education, and too often colouring their instructions with the vulgarity of their everyday life.

The high and dry type of clergy were the outcome of these first days of the restoration of the church to its old position in the country. Disgusted with the free and easy bearing of those who had usurped their places, the scholastic divines who had been brought up at the University, affected a stiff and starch mannerism socially, as well as in their preaching, and as time went on, the fervent and often intellectual Dissenting ministers began to prove formidable rivals to the clergy of the Established Church. The Dissenters' chapels, and even the Quakers' meeting-houses, were filled, while the churches were comparatively empty. This reaction from the irregularity of the Puritan services, to a dry and precise ritual, from which the life seemed to have died out, continued, till from the great evangelical fathers of the eighteenth century, which was now opening, arose the cry to the Spirit, to breathe on the dry bones and cause them to live.

Master Arthur Bedford was not a man of much learning, but he was cheerful and active. He threw himself with the greatest zest into Edward Colston's plans for the education of the boys in his parish, his faithful friend and ally. The relations between the vicar and the benefactor of the parish were most cordial, and as he sits at the hospitable board of the good Sir John Duddlestone, he is listening with pride and pleasure to the worthy knight's commendation of the boys in the Temple School.

"It has been good management there," he was saying. "Money won't buy good management and instruction, and I am bold to say that your reverence has borne a lion's share of the trouble of teaching."

"You do me honour, Sir John," Master Bedford said. "It is true I have had a pride in bringing the boys on, but I must not magnify my doings unduly. They tell me Master Colston will be here before long, to make a grand opening of the Great house. He is growing old, and I should not wonder if he made some relative a deputy to take his place."

"No, his fixed intention is to appear himself, and the time draws nigh. It is said that he wills to bring here with him the child he so greatly loves, but Mistress Ann Colston is too infirm to undertake such a long journey."

"And a perilous one, forsooth. I hear there was a daring robbery on Putney Heath not many days ago."

"Master Edward Colston seemeth to bear a charmed life," said Sir John, pushing the large silver tankard towards his guest. "He does not seem to come into misfortune like other folk, and to have a strange exemption from ills and troubles."

"So we think," said Master Bedford; "but we can only judge by appearances."

"That's well said," replied Sir John. "But I think, nevertheless, Colston has been marked out for prosperity and success; and if there is, as folks say, a general election in this coming autumn — well, our friend may stand and win."

"He would never consent at his advanced age to be put up for election."

"He would," replied Sir John, "if it were but to strengthen the hands of the Tories. He would stand, I say, for that end: and for my part, looking at the matter of Dr. Sacheverell, I cannot but confess that I see the Whigs have lost thereby."

Master Bedford rose, saying in a low voice :

"Great principles are at stake. It is somewhat rash to speak of them lightly. I must wish you good-day, Sir John, for I have my sermon in the Temple Church this evening."

"And a right good sermon I doubt not it will be, Master Bedford. But, look you, there are those that whisper even now, that you are touched with the colour and flavour of the Whigs. For myself I laugh at the notion— you who have worked so well hand-in-hand with Edward Colston—you who are put forward by him on all occasions—it is ridiculous to charge you with the Whig folly. A set of intriguing pig-headed people, who would pull down the whole country, and be buried in its ruins. We've had enough of pulling down, say I, and it's building up we want."

"True," replied Master Bedford, "only we ought to look to the foundations : if they are on the sand, no matter how fair the structure, the ruin is sure as great."

"Well, well, man ! Go and preach your

sermon, and take for your text, 'Fear God and honour the Queen,' and you won't be far wrong."

Master Bedford smiled, and went away, telling himself that if all those who hung out the colours of the Tories were as good men and honest as the worthy knight, and Edward Colston, the Whigs would not have much chance of winning in the contest.

"But alas! alas!" he exclaimed, "it is not so. It is no question with the great majority as to the good of their country, or the spread of religion, or the maintenance of peace. It is the struggle for power, and place, and name; and the many pay the penalty for the foolish vanity and greedy ambition of the few. I might have told Sir John as much; but he would not heed me. Good and true himself, he tries to think all men are like him."

As Master Bedford reached his own dwelling he was met by his sprightly wife, who had watched with some misgivings her husband's evident inclination towards those who had boldly expressed their sympathy with the Nonconformists in Bristol.

"You are late, husband; and methinks you should take some repose before preaching this night in the church. What news this is from London, that Dr. Sacheverell has in good sooth won a victory for the Church! Verily, I do rejoice, and Master Colston will be glad, indeed. Master Lane has been here, and he saith there will be an election of members for all the cities and boroughs in the country ere long, and that Master Colston may be put up as one willing to stand for Bristol."

"Women had best leave politics alone," was Master Bedford's reply. "These are days when every step of the way may lead the unwary into a pitfall. So, good wife, mind the house and the children, and talk not of things beyond thy province."

Mistress Bedford was not to be silenced so quickly. She talked on in a voluble strain of many rumours which had reached her ears, and finally she said, that Alderman Lane had more than hinted that Master Bedford was not deemed by many folk as orthodox, and that Master Edward Colston had not been well pleased at something Master Bedford had let fall in one of his lectures.

"Tut, tut! Let us hear no more old women's fables," was the answer. "It is the tongue which works half the mischief in this world, and nowhere is the mischief greater than in this city of Bristol. It may do me great harm if you give yours undue licence."

"Undue licence! It would do me harm if you lost your living, and I was turned out in the wide world with my poor babes." And then a shower of tears came to the relief of Mistress Bedford's excitement; while her husband, having put on his cassock, and taken his college cap from the peg where it hung, went forth to the lecture in the church, where the boys of the school sang Psalms for the service, and were afterwards questioned, according to the instructions of their benefactor, in the Church catechism.

It was one Friday morning in Lent when Edward Colston was crossing the path which skirted the common towards the church at Mortlake, to attend the service there, with his sister and his little niece. James, the black servant, walked behind bearing the books; and as the party passed along all hats were raised, and many bows and curtesies showed the respect in which the family was held; and nothing delighted little Say more than to smile and nod in return for these greetings. Sometimes Edward Colston stopped to inquire for the

MORTLAKE CHURCH.

health of some old man or woman, and now and then he took from the deep pockets of his long coat a book in which he made a note with a bit of pointed charcoal set in a silver case, the forerunner of the pocket pencil of later days.

The progress to the church was slow, and yet the bells were still chiming when the party entered the side door beneath the ancient tower now so thickly covered with ivy as to hide any outline of windows or tracery. There were very few worshippers. Mrs. Elizabeth Beavis and her daughter, with the servants from the rectory and a few poor old men and women from the almshouses, formed the congregation at first; but just as the first lesson was being read, steps were heard in the aisle, and a young man with a slight figure and easy bearing came up to one of the high pews, opened it, and sat down. As soon as the lesson was over and the clergyman began, "All ye works of the Lord, praise ye the Lord," the young man standing up, caught sight of those who occupied a large pew in the chancel. There, perched on one of the seats to bring her head on a level with the large prayer-book which rested on the ledge of the pew, was little Sarah Colston, one of her small hands resting on the open page, and the other held fast by her uncle, who turned from his book every now and then to watch the rapt expression of the child as she said the sentences in her pure silvery voice.

"O ye sun and moon, praise ye the Lord, praise Him and magnify Him for ever."

It was a beautiful picture—the grave old man with his large wig and richly embroidered surtout, with the child in her scarlet hood tied tightly under her round dimpled chin. They might have stood as a study for the painter—the child the type of the hundreds who in the future should bless the old man, who stood as the impersonation of the benevolence which has handed his name down for blessing in the city of his birth.

Mistress Ann Colston leaned heavily on her large gold-headed cane, and stood a little behind her brother and grand niece. She had no book, for she needed none. The services of the Church had been familiar to her from infancy, and she was only careful that little Say should follow the large print of her uncle's prayer-book, and repeat the words accurately.

The young stranger did not look at the book which was placed in his pew. As soon as the

Benedicite was over, he was buried in the depth of the high oak seat, and by the utmost craning of his neck, he could not catch a glimpse of anything in the chancel pew more interesting than the crown of Edward Colston's periwig.

But when the service was over, he watched his opportunity, and waited just outside the church till Edward Colston came up. It was a slow progress, for several pensioners were hovering about to catch the ear of Master Colston; but the young man advancing saw at last that he was recognized, and in another minute he had received a greeting more cordial than that which had been granted him, when he presented his mother's letter in the hall of Christ's Hospital.

He was then presented to—"My sister, Mistress Ann Colston," and to "my little niece, Sarah Colston," and was asked to return with the party to dine.

"Albeit, it is Friday in Lent, and there will only be a repast of fish and eggs, I think our good housekeeper can suit your palate, Master Aldworth."

Such an observance as the eating of fish on a Friday in Lent was new to the young man. Though a member of the Church, he had been born and brought up in Pennsylvania, under the shadow of that noble type of Quakerism, which was so widely different from the fanatical phase which we have seen prevailed in Bristol.

In Bancroft's history of the United States, there is a masterly sketch of these great Quakers, who, drifted by a storm of persecution to the other side of the Atlantic, were the founders of a goodly race of men and women, at liberty to believe and to pray according to their inspiration, in the free air of a new world, and who gathered in many souls by force of their pure and holy lives, as well as by their teaching."

"Fish is always good eating," Hyacinth Aldworth said. "I am not particular in my tastes, though one day is as another to me: Friday or Tuesday, it is all one."

Edward Colston became grave and serious at once.

"The Church, our reformed Church, sir, hath laid down certain laws for the maintenance of discipline and for the health of the souls of her members. To use godly abstinence in the season of Lent, is one of these, and I and my household are bound to obey. Scant blessing follows on scant obedience."

"What a stiff and starch old man he is!" thought Hyacinth Aldworth; "can he ever have been young? I did not want him to preach to me!"

When they had passed through the old stone gates leading into the grounds around the mansion, Edward Colston fell back a few paces and told Say to walk towards the house with her aunt, and that he would follow.

The child obeyed at once, and then Edward Colston said to Hyacinth Aldworth—

"I read your mother's letter in haste the other day. I have now read it at leisure, and suffice it to say, young sir, that I will do for you what she asks, and put you in the way of an honest livelihood by your hand or brain."

"I thank you, sir," was the reply with something of haughtiness in the tone. "Far be it for me to be a pensioner on your goodness. I wish for work, and having that, it will suffice."

Edward Colston turned and faced the young man. Here, at least, was not the spirit of his grandfather—the careless, pleasure-loving Hyacinth Sacheverell. Was it altogether fancy, that some likeness to one who had been at rest for many years, and was but distantly related to him, shone out of the boy's steadfast eyes?

"I honour you, sir, for seeking independence rather than to look for help. But as far as I can give the last, it shall be yours when needed. You may keep your terms at one of the Inns of Court, or you may resort to Oxford. It will give me pleasure to bear the cost."

The young man bowed and said, " Good sir, methinks if you are so benevolent as to put tools into my hands, you will soon discern that I will wield them to some purpose."

This was the beginning of a friendship which struck a root deeper into the life of the old man that any one guessed.

Young Aldworth became a frequent visitor at Mortlake. He was entered in the Temple, and soon showed the determination and energy which marks out a man for success.

From the first moment when he had caught sight of little Sarah perched upon the seat in the church, Hyacinth Aldworth had, as it were, appropriated the child as his friend, and to little Say, who had hitherto known no companions younger than Pepita and Mistress Ann Colston, there was a great charm in the bright sparkling society of this new friend. She looked forward to Saturday as a gala day, for then when she went to meet her uncle's barge, she was generally sure to see Hyacinth stepping out, and he always brought sunshine with him.

She would lead him all over the old house, and he would play hide and seek with her in the attic floor, and charm away her fear of Noll's secret chamber, by ascending the few stairs in the gable of the roof, and calling to her to follow, he would sing at the top of his young voice some snatches of a song, with the old Royalist chorus:—

"The King shall enjoy his own again."

Very cautiously and with much care, did little Say creep up the stairs to find Hyacinth, and though seizing his outstretched hand she said—

"Don't stay here, prythee. I always fear to see that wicked Oliver."

"There are two sides to Oliver. He was a great man on one side—a very great man."

"Oh!" said the child. "I can never, never speak to you any more if you call him great who murdered the blessed king."

Hyacinth smiled incredulously.

"That was an evil act, little one. Did I not tell you that the Protector had two sides?"

"Ah! but my Uncle Edward thinks he had

but one, and that one is a very fearful wicked one."

Again the young man smiled.

"Take care, Say, or we shall hear the old gentleman groaning. You know you told me he is heard here on winter nights. Hush!"

And as he spoke, the breeze of the June afternoon, which had come up the river, sighed through the crevices of the old rafters, and little Say, squeezing the hand of her companion, said

"Take me down! Oh! take me down!"

Then, ashamed of himself for playing upon the fears of the child, the young man carried her down the few rickety stairs, and they went to the long room called the Council Chamber, which was seldom used, except on the grand occasions when a number of City Magnates came from London, by barge or coach, to dine with Edward Colston.

The Council Chamber was panelled with oak, and there were pretty festoons of flowers all round the cornice of the vaulted roof.

There was a fire-place at the south end now filled with pots of fragrant shrubs, and on either side was a deep bay lattice window which looked out on the grounds.

This was a favourite resort with little Say, and she said to her companion, "Let us sit here and talk about my journey, for I am really going to Bristol with my Uncle Edward, and I shall see all his children go to the new house he has built for them, and I am to have gifts for them, and oh! it will be a grand day. You will come also."

"Nay, I think not, little one. You must bring me all the news, and when I have won my way up the steep ladder of learning, I will go to Bristol and see the house where my grandmother was born and where her sister Damaris died, all out of her care of my mother, who was lying sick of a fever."

"I have heard Pepita tell that story, but I did not know it was concerning you or those you knew of."

"I only know it by hearsay; but what I know is true, for my mother called a child of hers, my own little sister, after that lady, Damaris."

"You must talk to Pepita about it some day; she knows everything."

"Wonderful Pepita!"

"I mean about Bristol folks. She told me a story about a beautiful lady, who was the friend of this Mistress Damaris, whose lord was slain on Nugent Hill, not far from Uncle Edward's sister's house. And she lived for a hundred years a widow."

"Nay, now, my little Say. Not a hundred years, prythee; if so she must have been the widow of Methuselah."

"Ah! you are laughing at me," said the child; "perhaps it was fifty years. That is half one hundred, you know, and she might have married numbers of brave gentlemen; but no, she only cared for her dead lord, and she saved her wedding-dress for her shroud; and when she was buried Pepita's sister's son was in Bristol; and he heard music playing, and saw young girls with flowers, and, thought he, this is a wedding. And lo! it was the burial of Dame Pugsley, and not a wedding.

"Why," Say exclaimed, "there is Uncle Ned," and starting up she leaned out of the open casement, not six feet from the path below, and said—

"Ah! Uncle Edward, you have heard me telling my story of the burial of the poor lady."

"Aye, child, rather the story of her wedding; for did she not then rejoin her departed one to part no more?" Edward Colston turned away, and as his slow steps were heard on the terrace little Say sighed—

"How sad Uncle Edward looked! Dear Uncle Ned!"

THE GREAT HOUSE.

1710

That was a great day for little Sarah Colston when she set off in the roomy chariot for Bristol with her Uncle Edward.

The child's interest in what she should see and do, in the city of her ancestors, knew no bounds.

As the carriage, drawn by its four horses, passed along, through the towns and villages, her little earnest face might be seen at the window, remarking on everything she saw with the keenest interest.

Edward Colston's equipage was well known all along the route, and the hosts of the various inns, all testified to the honour they felt it, to provide for the wants of the travellers.

Within the carriage there were only Edward Colston and Sarah, with Pepita, who had accompanied the party to attend to the little lady; but in the rumble sat the negro James and another man-servant, both well-armed, for the roads were, after dark, very dangerous, by reason of highwaymen, who lurked in the unfrequented parts, and often stopped a carriage and rifled it of its contents with a speed which left little time for defence or resistance. Of these dangers Mistress Pepita was fully aware; but she kept her fears to herself, and it was a remarkable thing that in all his journeys to and from Bristol Edward Colston had never been attacked by robbers.

"The angel of the Lord is with them that fear Him, and put their trust in His mercy,' Mistress Ann Colston had said to herself as she watched the chariot roll down the smooth gravel drive. "Edward of all men may claim that promise."

Mistress Ann Colston's faith was not misplaced. On the evening of the third day the chariot stopped before the house in Small Street, where many members of the family were assembled, and little Say skipped lightly from the carriage into the wide hall, and was greeted by another child, also a great-niece of Edward Colston, who was to assist in the festivities of the 10th of July. She was older than little Say, and looked upon her as a baby to be in her especial charge. There were present in the hall at supper a goodly number of those who were glad to claim kindred with the merchant prince, who was, it might be said, like the head of a royal house, so highly was he esteemed by his relations and fellow-citizens.

Master Charles Brent, the rector of St. Werburgh's, was a cousin, and said grace at supper. Then there were several of the Edwards family, Mr. Edwards being Edward Colston's man of business, as well as connected with him by marriage, and the hospitalities of the Small Street mansion were kept up in a manner worthy of those which had preceded them in past years.

There was not a cloud in the sky on the 10th of July, when the streets of old Bristol were all alive with the approaching ceremony of opening the Great House on St. Augustine's Back.

Little Sarah and her cousin walked on either side of their uncle to the opening service in the cathedral; a flood of sunshine lighting the east end as the procession moved towards it, and the young faces of the boys, dressed in their quaint coats and stockings, were shining in the morning light.

After the boys, came Edward Colston and the

two children, little Say pressing her uncle's hand tightly in hers, and unwilling to part from him, when the solemn verger bowed him to the stall appropriated for his use by the Dean and Chapter.

The child's hesitation and clinging to her uncle were noticed, and while her cousin left him to take a seat appointed for the friends and relations of the Colston family, she was allowed to follow him to the stall, and was happy to sit unseen on a hassock at his feet, while the service went on, standing at the Psalms and Canticles, but quite lost to sight.

The Mayor, preceded by his cap of maintenance, and with Master Mason, head of the Merchant Venturers, and all the array of Aldermen and Councillors, made a grand show. No one of any importance in the city was absent, and the cathedral was crowded to the doors, many being unable to obtain admission.

As Edward Colston stood up in his place, and looked round upon the fruition of his hopes, and the fulfilment of a life's dream, he repeated with emphasis after the choir the last verses of the Psalms for the day, so strangely appropriate, that they brought the tears to many eyes, as they fell from the lips of the old man.

"As for me I am like a green olive tree in the house of God. My trust is in the tender mercy of God for ever and ever, and I will always give thanks unto Thee for that Thou hast done, and I will hope in Thy name, for Thy saints like it well."

When the service was over the procession was re-formed, and crossing the College Green, the bells of all the churches ringing a merry peal, it entered the great house, where in the principal hall, the school was formally opened, and all the happy boys filing past their good friend and patron, received from the children's hands gifts which had been carefully chosen and prepared by Edward Colston's order.

A banquet followed, and it was not till a late hour that Edward Colston was free to seek his own room, the same which he had always occupied in that house in early years.

Mistress Pepita was awaiting him, to inquire how he felt after his long and exciting day.

"Tired," he replied, "for seventy-five years is a weight to bear. Nevertheless I ought to have a light heart, good Pepita."

"Aye, indeed. There's many a tongue blessing you, my master, to-night in Bristol."

"How is the dear child, Pepita?"

NORMAN GATEWAY, COLLEGE GREEN.

"Asleep at last, dear lamb. She said, 'I would not like to abide in Bristol, Pepita. It maketh my head pain me. I like Mortlake best, and my cousin Sophia is mighty grand, and saith that she will have great riches when our uncle dies.'"

Edward Colston's eyes sparkled, and his lips parted as if to speak.

"Poor little Sophia! Is she then like the rest, counting on what will come when I am dead? Methinks those that expect nothing are blessed. Take care of our little Mortlake flower, in this large household, and see that she is not roughly dealt with, good Pepita, and now send James with my night draught; and so, with God's blessing on you, good-night."

When the excitement of the opening of the school in the Great House was over, and the business connected with it transacted, Edward Colston liked nothing better than to take his little grand-niece by the hand and show her the chief objects of interest in the old city of his birth.

These walks together were very different from those at Mortlake, and the bustle of the streets was sometimes too much for the child, when black James, who was her devoted servant, would raise her in his arms, and carry her through a busy thoroughfare till the space was cleared, to set her down by her uncle's side again.

One day they mounted together St. Michael's Hill by the celebrated steps which had been "newly steppered" a few years after the Restoration. Little Say was delighted to place herself in one of the curious stone seats at the top, and make her uncle take another, while James stood by showing his white teeth from ear to ear.

"1669," Sarah read from the tablet which recorded when the street was steppered, done, and finished. "That must have been when you were a little boy, Uncle Edward."

"Nay, child, forsooth, I was long past youth forty years agone. But we must hasten on to the almshouses, and speak to our kinsfolk there."

"Such dear little houses," Say said, as they passed through the iron gates to the square of turf beyond. "I would fain live in one when I grow old, Uncle Edward."

"It is a quiet spot, and peace reigns here. It is dear to me, child, as one of the first undertakings which God has blessed. See, this house on the right is where the Colstons live. They are of our kindred; but the stock from which they sprang was ever thriftless, and never bore much fruit. They have a safe asylum here."

THE ALMSHOUSES ON ST. MICHAEL'S HILL.

He tapped at the door, but there was no answer, for the inhabitants were out. A neighbour, however, appeared from the next house, and invited Master Colston into his dwelling.

Little Say was somewhat surprised to find that gratitude was not the prevailing feeling in these recipients of her uncle's bounty. A long story was told of scanty fuel, of a crack which let in cold air, of the disagreeable conduct of the next-door neighbour. Then there was a history of a cough which racked the speaker nigh and day, and of the money he had to pay for physic.

"It is to be hoped," Edward Colston said, as they left the almshouses, "that Thomas and George Colston fare better. They might go further and fare worse. But let us proceed."

"Nay, nay, dear Master Colston," another voice called. "I prythee enter my room, and let me have the honour of seeing you in the house you have provided for us old folks. I am a poor widow, and I was about to crave a favour of your honour."

Edward Colston paused, and said kindly to the woman who accosted him—

"What is it? Let me hear."

"That you would admit my boy—my only son—to your school. It would be a grace, indeed, and well bestowed."

"My good woman," said Edward Colston, resuming the stiff, cold manner which he always laid aside when talking to little Sarah, "I cannot promise rashly. I must examine into the case, and if I deem it a suitable one, I will crave leave of the excellent chief of the Merchant Venturers to be your boy's patron. Is that the boy?"

For now, from behind a door opening into

the back premises of the almshouses, appeared a round, roguish face. The figure was hidden, and only one chubby hand was visible as it grasped the half-open door.

"Come forward, you ill-mannered Jack-in-the-box!" was the woman's summary order, "and make your dutiful reverence to this grand gentleman, who has been the saving of your poor aged grandfather's life, and will now be the making of yours."

Some rather rough expressions of maternal affection followed in the shape of cuffs on the head and a smart slap on the back. But at last the boy was kneeling on one knee before Edward Colston.

"Thank your great benefactor," said the mother.

"No, no!" said Edward Colston, who had taken the large oak chair just within the cottage and drawn little Sarah upon his knee. "No, no, teach your son better than that. Verily we do not thank the clouds for rain, nor the sun for light; but we thank God who made both the clouds and the sun. I will see to the boy's future, always supposing that I hear no ill report of him or his mother."

"His grandfather, Josiah Walsh, was one

of the first inhabitants of the almshouses—a respectable man—ay, and a grateful one to boot, your honour. I, a poor widow, his daughter, can swear to that."

Edward Colston paid but little heed to the mother, but he beckoned the son to come nearer, and then put him through a course of questions which only served to show his ignorance.

Little Sarah, of seven—precocious and as forward in learning as many children of twice her years was amazed at the stupidity of this aspirant for a place in the school.

As she trotted away by her uncle's side, she said—

"Was there ever such a dunce as that boy? He seemed to know scarce his own name; and as to who gave him his name, he looked like one in a dream when he was asked the question."

"Ay, indeed, and there are many hundreds in the city like him. But, child, I see better days coming, when these boys of mine shall be grown men, and teach their boys and girls the value of learning, which is greater than silver and gold. But I must see Master Mason on this matter on the morrow. We shall find him at the house in St. Peter's Churchyard, where the corporation of the poor holds its deliberations. But this is enough for to-day. I am weary, and we must turn our steps homewards, but we will pass under St. John's Gateway, which so greatly amazed and pleased the good Queen Elizabeth on her visit to the City."

This was but one of many walks about the old city which provided little Sarah with many pictures to be reproduced by her in her lonely life at Mortlake, as she played in the old Council Chamber, or climbed on

ST. JOHN'S GATE.

the benches of the summer-house to look out from one of the little windows for the return of the barge from London.

Her uncle took a delight in showing her All Saints' Church, where his kindred lay, and when he said—"Here, child, do I hope my bones will lie," she answered, " And I would fain lie with you here, Uncle Edward. I should not like a lonely grave."

"Ah! dear child, your time is far off. I pray God you may live to be the joy and comfort of many hearts."

"I should like to be the joy of yours," she said, with that fond pressure of her uncle's hand he loved to feel.

The return journey began early in August, and little Sarah slept for the greater part of it. She was tired with all she had seen, and her faithful Pepita said truly that she had not only wearied her body but her mind, and that if she had stayed much longer in Bristol she would never have left it alive.

"The child is not fitted for the bustle and the noise. I'll be thankful when we are safe at home," she said.

It was a sultry August day when the last stage of the journey was reached, and the travellers were much oppressed with heat.

Clouds were gathering on the horizon, and every now and then a low murmur of thunder was heard and a flash of lightning struck across the round tower of Windsor Castle, as they stopped in the town, for the last bait of the horses.

"Put on your speed," Edward Colston said to the post-boys, "for the days are shortening fast, and night will overtake us ere we see the tower of Mortlake Church." As he spoke from the window of the carriage, a large drop of rain fell on his face and another flash of lightning shining on little Sarah's face, she awoke and sat up.

"Was that the shining of Aunt Ann's lamp, Pepita?"

"No, no, my lamb; we are not home yet, worse luck. It is a storm brewing; and I never can abide to be out of doors in thunder."

Edward Colston made room for the child next him, saying, "Do not alarm the little one. We are safe under the feathers of the Almighty One, here as in our own house;" and nestling close to her uncle, little Sarah fell off to sleep again.

The carriage went on as quickly as bad roads permitted, for to shorten the distance the postilion had turned off the main highway, and taken a shorter and less frequented road, which skirted Richmond Park, and came out below Putney Heath.

It was more haste and less speed, for the stoppages were many, caused by obstacles, to remove which, the servants in the rumble had to get down several times.

Now a small heap of stones; now a fallen branch of a tree; now a hurdle; and once the dead body of a lean and miserable horse, lay across the way.

The shadows were gathering, and though the storm had not as yet broken overhead, the heavy clouds in the west darkened the sky and shut out what daylight yet lingered.

"We should have been better advised than to take this route. We have travelled by it before, it is true; but that was when the March winds had dried the country-side, and the mud and mire were not so deep as now. There must have been a great rainfall in these parts; but we are coming out from under the trees soon, and then it will be better."

As he spoke, there was a sudden stoppage of

the horses, a cry from the servants, and in a moment two men with masks put their faces in at the windows of the chariot, and a voice said:

"Your purse or your life!"

"Come, come, good sir," said another, "my fellow is somewhat sharp and short. Have the goodness to hand us a few of your valuables, and we will let you pass!"

Edward Colston did not lose his presence of mind. He bid the terrified housekeeper be quiet, and not add to the tumult by screams, while he held his little niece close in his arms and said:

"My masters, I am an honest man, and I will not give up my money at the word of thieves and robbers."

"We'll see to that," said the first speaker, and the click of a loaded musket was distinctly heard.

"Come, hand us out your purse, good sir, and I will ensure your safety. The men at the horses' heads are mine. At my word they will release their hold and you will go on. Now, good sir, I do not care to parley here till midnight."

"If, as I take it from your voice and manner, sir, you come of gentle birth, I cry shame on you for stopping an old man of seventy-five, a child of scarce seven years, and a defenceless woman, on the Queen's highway. I will not aid, abet, or encourage you in your evil manner of life. I trust in God, who has preserved me in my journeyings hitherto, and I trust him still."

" Ha, ha! you are of that sort!" said the first speaker, with an oath; "but why parley longer?"

Suddenly the hand which was on the carriage door released its hold, and the dark figure fell back into the road, while the horses, evidently struggling to be free, rocked the carriage violently from side to side. There was a minute of desperate confusion, voices shrieking, the sound of heavy blows, while above all rang a voice which was familiar.

"Press on, my boys. Drive on. Down with the rascals," and Hyacinth Aldworth, with a well-directed blow, freed the door of the carriage from the grasp of the second highwayman, and leaping into his place on the wide step, he said in a re-assuring tone: "We are safe now, thank God. The two leaders of the gang are lying in the road, and two men I brought with me have put the others to flight."

"No lives are lost, I pray," Edward Colston said.

"No: though I am not so chary of those fellows' lives to make much moan if they are stopped from further mischief. To attack the defenceless is sure a crime worthy of punishment."

"Vengeance is mine," replied Edward Colston solemnly; "I will repay, saith the Lord; but there is my little niece trembling like a leaf, and I pray you, good Pepita, open the locker below the seat and find her a cordial; nor scream, now that danger is past. My people, James and Harry, and the post-boys, are they safe?"

"I think so. James had a pretty sharp blow, and Harry a cut with a knife, but they will hold over, till we reach home."

"You are our brave deliverer. How did it come about?"

"That is a long story, and must be related more at length anon. Suffice it now to say, that as I was passing from the bridge at Putney this forenoon, on my way to inquire of Mistress Ann Colston if she had tidings of you, I heard words let fall at an Inn, into which I turned for refreshment, which enlightened me that this was the last day of your journey from Bristol, and that a plot was laid to intercept you hard by the three cross ways, at the turn of the Sheen road, and relieve you of great treasures, which it was said you were bringing home to Mortlake. They called you the Prince of Merchants, and by no other name, but it did not need much wit to find them out. Hence I armed myself, and four hearty men commended to me after the rascals left, by mine host, and we have been lying in wait, creeping on hands and knees amongst the furze bushes and bracken, and brambles, till at last we came on those we sought. I felled him on the right, and, as you know, soon did the same office for the other to the left, while the men grappled with the rest; and that is my story."

"Give God the praise," said Edward Colston, "first, and then, noble boy, receive mine, for saving our lives by your well-directed and heroic conduct."

Hyacinth Aldworth had opened the chariot door at the beginning of his story, and was now seated next Pepita, who could by no means restrain her hysterical cries, and declared with tears that Say was dead.

"Nay, nay, she is but insensible. It is a terrible shock. Give her to me," said the young man, "and let the pure air blow on her."

This very sensible advice was followed, and little Sarah soon opened her eyes.

The light of the lanthorn flashed on her pale face; but a smile played upon her lips as she recovered.

"We are quite safe now *you* are here, Master Hyacinth."

The story was told at Mortlake with as little detail as possible, for Mistress Ann Colston could not control her agitation on hearing the bare facts. Indeed, for her sake and for little Sarah's, the subject was seldom referred to in the household. Pepita denying herself the pleasure of relating it with all its horrors, lest she should hurt the young child and the old lady, whose nerves were alike unable to bear the thought of the peril which had been escaped.

Edward Colston had every means taken to bring the highwaymen to justice; but it was supposed that the blows had only stunned them, and that they had soon recovered and escaped, as nothing was heard of them.

"They have as many lives as a cat, these gentlemen of the road. They are as slippery as eels, and are here, there, and everywhere, like wills-o'-the-wisp," so said Mistress Elizabeth Beavis, when she was talking over the events of that memorable drive from Windsor with Mr. Jones. "It is the first time that ever I heard of any evil-disposed fellows attacking Master Colston. But the young deliverer has become like a son of the house, and no doubt will benefit hereafter. So it is an 'ill wind that blows nobody good;' and that young Aldworth will find out."

FOR WHIG OR TORY?

POLITICAL excitement was at its height in Bristol in October of this year. The appeal to the country was felt to be of more than usual importance. 'The Church and Dr. Sacheverell,' was the watchword of the Tories, and there were not wanting those in Bristol who echoed the cry, shouting it till they were hoarse, and thus proclaiming the changed political bias of the once Puritan Council Chamber far and near. Changed, indeed, it was to all outward appearance, and the successors of Skippon and those who had deposed Creswicke and William Colston from their high office as mayor and alderman were of a different type. The voice of the city now clamoured for Tory representation in the new House of Commons, and it was thought that the man who had been so great a benefactor to Bristol would be certain to carry a large majority, as many would vote for him, not so much from party motives as from personal regard.

"We are sure of the clergy to a man," good Sir John Duddlestone said, as he looked up at the High Cross, which had been painted and gilded in honour of her gracious Majesty's visit to Bristol five years before. "We are sure of the clergy to a man, and I'll e'en go and consult Master Bedford at the Temple, for he will do us good service by canvassing for votes in his district."

The little alert man to whom these words were addressed gave a short laugh. He was Mr. Secretary Burchett, who for his services to the committee of Captain Earle and Master Edward Colston, had a gross of bottles of sherry presented to him a few months later!

"Do you take your opinion of the reverend Master Bedford from the top of the High Cross, Sir John? Methinks, you are looking there for what you will fail to find, if it be so."

"I may stare at the Cross if I choose," said Sir John, bluntly. "I always like to see it glistening in the sunshine as now. It reminds me of something above all this strife and warfare."

The two men were on the steps before the Council Chamber, which had been lately rebuilt. Many Bristol magnates were passing up and down, and everyone was discussing the same subject. The poll was to be opened in a few days, and the usual expedients were resorted to, to win the votes of the people. The proclamation to call the new Parliament had been issued on September 26th, and no time was to be lost.

"Master Colston has refused point blank to stand for the city," said the Mayor, Mr. Christopher Shuter, touching Sir John on the shoulder. "He has determined that his age is too great, and pleads it as an excuse."

"Nevertheless," said Mr. Burchett, "he shall be put up. If we are to succeed in Bristol it must be by his means."

"Well, well, I think Earle a very pretty candidate and a moderate man, who will please some folks more than Master Colston, who is stiff as a poker as to some points, where I say there should be freedom," said Mr. Sheriff Host.

"Tut, tut, man. Do not cry down your own cause like that. It is time to be stiff for the Queen and the Church, or mayhap we shall be in the thick of another crisis, and the low sort of fellows will ride over us roughshod, as in times not so long agone, either.

"Well, well, I am off to find one strong supporter, so I hope, and there is no time to let the grass grow under our feet, I can tell you, good folks. The other side are busy as bees amongst wild thyme."

"Say, rather, as rats in their holes, Sir John," was Mr. Burchett's remark, as the worthy knight went away. He was not so secure as he professed to be of Mr. Bedford's allegiance. To be sure, as on a previous occasion a few weeks before, he spoke as if he took it for granted that the man, who owed so much to Edward Colston would give him a hearty co-operation in his new departure, but he felt that Mr. Bedford's rejoinder had been doubtful. Sir John's spacious mansion was in the parish of St. Werburgh, and as he passed it on his way to the Temple he was stopped by one of his men.

"There is a messenger from Mortlake, Sir John, who has ridden post-haste with a despatch from Master Edward Colston."

Sir John hastily opened the letter and read, not without difficulty, its contents. For the good knight had perhaps more appreciation of the benefits of education, which his friend had conferred on the rising generation of Bristol, by reason of the deficiency of his own. After knitting his brows and pursing up his lips, breathing heavily all the time as if he were going through great bodily as well as mental exercise, he made out the letter to his satisfaction.

It was to the effect that the old man of seventy-five begged Sir John Duddlestone to entreat his good friends in the city to select another candidate at the forthcoming election of members. He had, he said, publicly notified his wish to Mr. Secretary Burchett, but he felt that he must appeal to Sir John to see it carried out.

"No, no; he only shrinks from it from his native modesty. The cause will be weakened if not ruined, if he is not put up. Good friend, Edward Colston, in this I cannot do your bidding. Stand you must, and stand you will, as a man. Here," he went on, turning to his servant, "tell the messenger to eat his fill and rest to-night, and on the morrow I will send a return letter to Master Colston."

Then he pursued his way to the Vicarage without further delay.

When he reached the house he was met by Mistress Bedford. She had a child in her arms, and another was hanging to her gown.

"Good-day to you, Mistress," said Sir John, chucking the baby under the chin, a little too roughly for its equanimity, for a squall which his mother tried to smother, was the result.

"Where is your good husband, Mistress Bedford?"

"I pray you, Sir John, step in, and I will call my husband. Here, Bet," she exclaimed, to a girl of fourteen, "take the children, or your father will rate me for their crying, and keep them quiet. For, Sir John, my husband is not like himself. He is cross-grained, and, like touch-wood, he flames up at a spark. It is these times which trouble him. I would the election had never been thought of. What's it to me whether the Whigs or the Tories please Her Majesty? It's all a parcel of farrago, and then plain English is, every man for himself, and the higher he pushes himself the better."

While Mistress Bedford was speaking, she was leading Sir John to the room at the end of a long passage, where they found the Vicar sitting with books and papers, on the table before him.

It was a low dark room, wainscotted with oak, and two small windows with high window-sills looked out on the Temple churchyard.

Mr. Bedford rose, and pushing back his hair

from his forehead with a weary gesture, he greeted Sir John respectfully.

"Aye! at your books then, Master Bedford! verily, you look as if you needed respite from learning and teaching. I have come to have a word with you touching the election. You are so quiet here, you must be apt to forget the busy city within a stone's throw."

"I pray you be seated, Sir John," Master Bedford said; "and you, wife, go and find something under our poor roof wherewith Sir John may refresh himself."

But Mistress Bedford, who had pricked up her ears at the word 'election,' lingered, saying—

"Election mad all the town hath gone! and more fools they."

"Hush, wife," said Master Bedford sternly; "such words are unbecoming; go and attend to your duties in the house. You must pardon her, Sir John. She is excited beyond measure on this matter, of which, poor soul, she knows nothing."

"It seems to me Mistress Bedford has many in the city who are companions in this. But look you, Master Bedford, we need your help. Your own vote is secure for Edward Colston;

but try, I pray you, to gain others to our mind."

"I deal not in bribes, Sir John. I would not tempt any man to go against his conscience by a bribe of money or wine."

"As if I thought on such a thing! but there are other ways—you can speak—no man better; you can bring before folk, how great a benefactor would represent them in parliament. You could by that means further the cause of the Church and the Queen as few men could. And," said Sir John, slapping his knee emphatically, "we look to you to do it. You who hold a benefice in the Church—you, who owe Mr. Colston as much as any man. So, sir, I say, we look for your help in this matter."

"Sir John," said Master Bedford, "I crave your pardon if I ask to be excused from entering on so weighty a matter as this; nor do I desire to declare here, at this time, my course of action, or my reasons for taking that course."

Sir John rose with an impatient gesture.

"I have no time to parley. Look you, sir— I ask a plain question: will you give your vote and your support, by getting other votes, for Mr. Edward Colston, who is to stand for this ancient city of Bristol?"

Sir John's voice and manner grew more and more vehement, and Mr. Bedford's calmer and more self-restrained. His deep-set eyes flashed a little from under his strongly marked brows, but he rose as Sir John did from his seat, and said—

"I leave Bristol to-morrow to tarry for awhile with relations in Gloucester, and thus, sir, I shall not be present at the poll of which you speak."

"Then I cry shame on you, sir," said Sir John with vehemence. "And I counsel you to look into the meaning of the word friend, and take it to heart, lest you forsake your best friend when he needs you most."

"I am not sure that he does so need me. A man who has counted seventy and five years, may surely demand an immunity from public service."

"That is a trickster's answer, sir. No, no," Sir John exclaimed, as Mistress Bedford returned, bringing him some spiced canary and delicate wheaten bread on a salver. "No, no, I can drink nothing here. Your pardon, Mistress Bedford, but I am sorely grieved by the conduct of one I deemed a friend. I wish you good-day—both of you—and I would fain hope that the morrow may find you in a better mind."

These were Sir John Duddlestone's last words, and he marched off with the air of an offended man, leaving Mr. Bedford and his wife together, the untouched wine and refreshment on the table,

A LAUREL CROWN.

"I PRAY thy uncle may have a safe journey," Mistress Ann Colston said, one dull November afternoon, with an anxious glance at the old clock which stood in a corner of the blue drawing-room. "His coming will be surely marked, as a Member of the Queen's Parliament, even more now than before; and I dread to think of the evil disposed lying in wait for him."

"Nay, Aunt Nan, did you not always say Uncle Edward was under the care of the Almighty? and though we were stopped on the road in August, none were hurt. That showed the care of the Father in Heaven for us."

"Dear child, that is true. I stand rebuked by thy faith."

"And another good thing that came from our fright was Hyacinth's brave deed; and now he is like our very own."

"Aye, truly; but he will soon be leaving us for America—and he is in duty bound if his mother needs him."

"How the wind sweeps through the trees! there is scarce a leaf left, and the light is fading fast. I would I could hear the wheels of the carriage! I am very hard of hearing now."

Little Say was perched on a high stool by the window, her face pillowed on her small hands, and her eyes gazing out across the wide lawn round which the drive swept from the old stone gateway. The few leaves left by November blasts, were chasing each other across the grass, and the spreading cedar proudly waved its dark green foliage in the chill wind, as if to flaunt its superiority over the less hardy elms and beeches, which were now nearly stripped bare of every leaf.

At last the longed-for carriage came in sight, and there were sounds of cheers and the tread of many feet.

For the Mortlake people were fired with the political excitement of the times, and though it is certain that the Bristol benefactor was not as popular at Mortlake as in his native city, they had come out to meet him on his return as Member for Bristol, and would have taken out the horses and carried him to the house in triumph, had he not begged to be excused on the score of age.

For in truth, Edward Colston was much worn out with the excitement of the last few weeks. He had been chosen to stand for the City of Bristol without his formal consent, and the result of the poll had surprised everyone. A majority was hoped for, but not a majority of a thousand votes!

As the chariot wound slowly up the drive and stopped before the door, Edward Colston stood up and bowed with all his old stately graciousness to the crowd. Then he thanked them in a few words for their welcome, and descending from the carriage passed into the hall where little Say and his aged sister were awaiting him.

Master William Jones, Mrs. Elizabeth Beavis, and Hyacinth Aldworth, all arrived for supper, and though Edward Colston looked tired and jaded, when the meal was over he gave them the account they desired of the proceedings at Bristol, for he had only written one short letter during his absence, and increasingly disliked, as he said, 'putting his pen to paper.'

He had a slow but graphic manner in describing events, and Mistress Nan Colston being placed with her best ear near her brother's chair, and little Sarah at his feet, he began :—

"And you are all anxious to hear of the honours done me at Bristol. In good sooth, they were greater than I had any reason to expect. Not only was the number of those who elected me very large, but the goodwill shown made every vote worth ten to me."

"And did you not feel sick and squeamish when carried in the chair?" little Sarah asked.

"Somewhat, but they dealt gently with me as an aged man. It was a sight, sister, to bring back many memories. The whole city wore its gayest aspect, and St. Werburgh's bells were echoed by the bells of all the churches.

"The autumn sky was clear above my head, and as I gazed up at the tower of All Saints, over which a few white clouds were floating, I thought of the Saints in Paradise, whom you and I, sister, shall by God's grace, soon join."

His voice trembled a little, and the old brother and sister clasped hands with a sudden impulse.

"Yes, I thought of our father and mother in heaven, and of the seventy-six years which have passed like a shadow since they carried me for baptism to the Temple Church; and when I saw my boys with their rosy happy faces cheering lustily, and the good old fellows from the Almshouses, and the aged sailors and the children from Temple School come out to see the show, my heart was too full of joy, and I found its spring lies very near the fountain of tears!"

He paused, and little Say drew closer to him and laid her cheek against his knee.

Years might come and go, and an ocean roll between that quiet blue drawing-room at Mortlake and Hyacinth Aldworth's distant home; but he could never forget the picture as it was then graven on his memory for ever.

"I was near in spirit," Edward Colston continued, turning his head towards Hyacinth, "to one who is of kin to you, young man. I alone knew that the goodly harvest which God has suffered me to reap was sown by her hand. Her voice came back to me over the waste of years. Her words were these: 'Therein lies the strength of the future, that the people should be well taught; for how many, I pray you to consider, err from sheer ignorance!'"

Again there was a pause, broken only by the crackling of the logs on the wide hearth and the howling of the wintry wind in the chimney. The old man heard none of these sounds; his ears were open to the tones of that musical voice, long since hushed in death, the summer breeze making a sweet harmony with it in the woods of Leigh, the gentle ripple of the water below, the distant shout of the boys' mellow laughter.

"'So far and yet so near,'" he murmured; but no one heard what he said.

Presently he roused himself, and answered many questions from his neighbours as to the election.

"Yes," he said, "the election has shown me who are my friends, and there was but one of them who showed himself my opponent."

"Not Master Bedford, brother?"

"Yes, sister Ann, it is even so." And now those thin lips curled with the bitter smile, which so entirely changed the expression of his face.

"Yes, the Rector of the Temple departed to Gloucester."

"That city of rebels always," interposed Master Jones.

"To Gloucester, to escape the poll in Bristol. That were ill done, seeing that it was his friend and coadjutor of years for whom the slight service was asked. But sure it was worse to vote for one in that city, who is not only touched with the flavour of the Whigs, but is of the fanatical and sectarian party, which will assuredly, unless all good Churchmen buckle on their armour, gain the victory over all order, loyalty, and peace in the realm. Of Master Arthur Bedford I desire to speak no more; our connection is severed, and I must warn the trustees of the Temple School that their minister has continually sided with those who are the enemies of peace. He has wounded me deeply; but that is a small matter when weighed in the balance with betrayal of his Church and his sovereign lady the Queen."

Edward Colston spoke proudly and bitterly.

"But you will forgive him, Uncle Edward; you will forgive Master Bedford?"

A gentle pat upon little Sarah's cheek was the only reply to her words; but, though lying buried for a season, they bore fruit.

"Did you sit in your beautiful stall in the Cathedral, Uncle Edward?" Sarah asked presently.

"Yes, dear child, and I bore in mind the little woman who would fain take the highest place in July last."

"Nay, now, Uncle Edward, it was the lowest; for I sat at your feet," she said, promptly.

"All my children were present at the service last Sunday, and I wished you could have been there, sister, to see them file past orderly and reverently to their seats."

"Ay, dear, I shall never set foot in Bristol again. My kinsfolk must come and visit me now," was the reply.

"There are great improvements of late in the city, so I hear," said Mrs. Beavis. "I have a cousin who lives in St. Peter's Churchyard, and she writes word that the face of the city is so changed, that, save for the churches and the steep Pithay, and the Christmas Steps, she might well believe that she was in another place, not in Bristol at all."

"Nay, that is drawing too strong a picture," said Edward Colston: "doubtless there are changes, and, we must concede, improvements. The brick buildings on the Broad Quay have a fine frontage, the new Merchants' Hall is grand, and the laying-out of College Green is a vast improvement, as is also the taking down of the hulks of the old houses on the Bridge. Then there is scarce a finer cross in

THE PITHAY.

England than the High Cross—now it has been painted and gilded."

"Dear heart," said Mistress Ann Colston, "I cannot bring myself to think of the bridge without the houses. Well do I remember how our dear mother would lead us along when children at Christmas-tide, to see all the brave show of foreign goods there, the finest to be met with in the city, to say nothing of the clocks with their strange devices. Ah! it seems time for the old to go when so many old things are passing."

"But we must not forget," Hyacinth Aldworth said, "that the old must give way to the new order, and that we must not impede progress."

"Have a care, young man," said Edward Colston, "nor trench too far on the ground of the enemy. It is the pulling down of old landmarks which has wrought so much mischief in the country."

"Many old things are beautiful," Hyacinth said, bowing to Mistress Ann Colston with a grace which recalled his grandfather; "but surely none can say useless hulks of houses are not better swept away!"

"Well, we will not contest it," was Edward

Colston's reply. "And now the hour is late, and this little maid is nearly asleep."

"Carry me up to Pepita, Hyacinth," little Sarah said, holding out her arms with childlike confidence.

"Indeed I will," said the young man, "but I must be paid for my trouble."

He raised her in his strong arms, and kissing him on the cheek, she said archly:

"Is that your pay?"

"Nay, it must be threefold," he replied, as he let her stoop down from his arms to kiss her uncle and aunt and Mrs. Beavis.

"Not Master Jones," she said; "no, he tries to take a kiss without leave; he steals it, and uncle Edward says, 'Never reward a thief!'"

"What a child it is!" exclaimed Master Jones, laughing heartily; but Mistress Ann Colston said:

"A pert tongue must be checked, or good manners will suffer."

"Nay, now, Mistress Colston, she is but a baby."

"The more need to curb her tongue in time," was the reply.

"Young Aldworth is as a son in this house," said Edward Colston, "and helps us to spoil the child; but my sister is right. We must check anything like discourtesy, be it in play or earnest; but truly the child is as the light of the eyes in this household, where we are all entering into the shadows of advancing age. We shall be losing young Aldworth before long, I fear me: his mother pines for him, and clearly his first duty is to her. A man can never have but one mother," he added, with a sigh; "and when that tie is broken the end does not seem far distant. So at least have I felt as regards mine; nor do I grudge any dutiful tenderness I may have shown her now. Rather does it all seem too poor and small in the retrospect."

"Then how poor and small must my service look," sighed Mistress Ann Colston.

THE RETURN.

1720.

In the dim shadow of a late October afternoon Hyacinth Aldworth found himself, after the lapse of some years, once more standing in the hall of the house at Mortlake, where he had spent so many happy hours in times past. He had returned to his mother after three years' study in England, which Edward Colston had provided for him, and he had stayed with her to the end of a somewhat sorrowful life.

He had made himself a place and a name in Pennsylvania, whither he hoped to return; and he had undertaken this voyage to England (then, as we know, considered a long and perilous one) solely to see his friend and benefactor once more.

Letters had passed, it is true, between them at rare intervals. As age advanced, Edward Colston disliked more and more to use his pen; and Hyacinth's chief correspondent had been

Sarah, the child he had left, now grown into a fair and most womanly maiden of nearly seventeen; but she, too, had been silent for some time.

Pepita had admitted him and had recognized him at once. "There are many changes, Master Aldworth," she said. "The dear old mistress is gone, the master is feeble, though his mind is clear, and the dear child is—"

"She is well, she is here?" Hyacinth exclaimed.

"She is here, but well—no. It makes my heart ache to say it; but I believe the dear master will see her laid in the grave before him."

Hyacinth tried to make light of the good housekeeper's words.

"No, no; you are living here a dull life, Mistress Pepita, and take a gloomy view of things. I'll soon cheer you up. We will hope on—hope ever."

"Ay, you are young; but it is hard for the old to hope; not that I am so very old either," said Pepita, who was sensitive in the matter of age; "but it is a doleful thing to watch the going down of those you love, and feel no hand can save them, and as to that child, from her Uncle who dotes on her, down to the scullery maid, she is just worshipped here, and that's the

THE RETURN.

1720.

In the dim shadow of a late October afternoon Hyacinth Aldworth found himself, after the lapse of some years, once more standing in the hall of the house at Mortlake, where he had spent so many happy hours in times past. He had returned to his mother after three years' study in England, which Edward Colston had provided for him, and he had stayed with her to the end of a somewhat sorrowful life.

He had made himself a place and a name in Pennsylvania, whither he hoped to return; and he had undertaken this voyage to England (then, as we know, considered a long and perilous one) solely to see his friend and benefactor once more.

Letters had passed, it is true, between them at rare intervals. As age advanced, Edward Colston disliked more and more to use his pen; and Hyacinth's chief correspondent had been

Sarah, the child he had left, now grown into a fair and most womanly maiden of nearly seventeen; but she, too, had been silent for some time.

Pepita had admitted him and had recognized him at once. "There are many changes, Master Aldworth," she said. " The dear old mistress is gone, the master is feeble, though his mind is clear, and the dear child is—"

"She is well, she is here?" Hyacinth exclaimed.

"She is here, but well—no. It makes my heart ache to say it; but I believe the dear master will see her laid in the grave before him."

Hyacinth tried to make light of the good housekeeper's words.

"No, no; you are living here a dull life, Mistress Pepita, and take a gloomy view of things. I'll soon cheer you up. We will hope on—hope ever."

"Ay, you are young; but it is hard for the old to hope; not that I am so very old either," said Pepita, who was sensitive in the matter of age; "but it is a doleful thing to watch the going down of those you love, and feel no hand can save them, and as to that child, from her Uncle who dotes on her, down to the scullery maid, she is just worshipped here, and that's the truth. I wish she weren't so like an angel, then I'd feel more cheerful about her."

"What is wrong with her?" asked Hyacinth Aldworth. "What is her ailment?"

"Ah! what indeed? you can see for yourself, Master Aldworth. Go in quietly or you will startle them. They are both in the blue drawing-room, for the dear old master affects that room more than any other."

Hyacinth crossed the hall, and opening the door softly, stood for a moment uncertain whether he should speak before he advanced further.

Edward Colston was reclining in a large chair. His figure was partly in shadow, but his face, turned in profile towards Hyacinth, was illuminated by the bright blaze of the wood fire on the hearth. There was a large chair opposite to Edward Colston's, but it was empty. There Mistress Ann Colston had sat for many years, and it was held sacred to her memory, and never occupied; but close to it was a couch with a number of coverings and soft cushions piled on it, almost in Eastern fashion, and there, half lying, half sitting, was the figure of a girl dressed in a thick wadded wrapper, and hanging from her shoulders was a musk-coloured velvet mantle lined with squirrel-fur. The sleeves beneath the loose wrapper were tight, and lace frills drooped over the slender fingers, which held a book between them in a listless fashion, for Sarah was not reading, but gazing dreamily into the fire.

The lovely head rested against a crimson cushion, which made a background to the beautiful lily-whiteness of neck and throat, encircled by a white tippet, with a lace frill turned back from the front, but rising behind ruffle-wise. The geranium colour of her lips, and the spot of a still more vivid hue upon either cheek, heightened her beauty, and told their own story to practised eyes ; but not to Hyacinth Aldworth. He only saw before him a beautiful woman in the place of the child he had left behind him, and he could see no symptoms of the dangerous condition about which the housekeeper had spoken. As Hyacinth waited, lost in admiration by the picture before him, Sarah raised her head, sat upright, and caught sight of him.

" Hyacinth !" she exclaimed at once, and then with a cry of delight, she said :

" Uncle Edward ! he is come at last."

The old man turned slowly in his chair, and holding out his hand, said : "Ah! welcome, Master Aldworth. I began to fear I should see your face no more, for the sands of life are running low." Sarah had drawn near Hyacinth, and he had involuntarily held out his arms to her: it seemed like an instant recognition on both sides. He had found his child-love grown into a woman, and she had found that the dream of her young maidenhood was fulfilled. The sudden revelation and joy, however, made her draw back, and the colour on her face gave way to a marble pallor, to be succeeded almost immediately by a burning blush.

When they had parted Sarah was a child of ten. Seven years had gone by, and she was a woman now, and she knew it.

"Nay, Say, my little Say," he murmured, "are you not glad to see me?"

"Ask Uncle Edward," she said, rallying herself, "and say something to him. Have you left your courtesy on the other side of the ocean. Fie! I must put you to study the 'Tatler' and 'Spectator.' You will see then how brave gentlemen should behave."

She talked on, to hide her real emotion. Her eyes were luminous, and her whole manner so bright, that Hyacinth could not for a moment take a gloomy view of her health. But the next day he noticed a short cough, not loud, but persistent. He saw, too, that when she took him upstairs to see "Oliver's room," she caught her breath suddenly, and put her hand to her side. But before he had been in the house a week, he had confided to Edward Colston that the love he had always felt for the child, had deepened into love for the woman, and that if he disapproved of his telling Sarah the truth, he would leave Mortlake, for stay there and be silent, he could not.

The old man shook his head.

"Alas," he said, "there is no wedding-gown for her. The physicians are all agreed that her days will be few; but if you must needs tell her of your love, I cannot say you nay. All our kindred who come hither take the gloomiest view of the child's continued ill-health. Mary Edwards and Nancy Colston told me not a month ago that she would never see another spring."

"But why should they be right? rather, why should they not be wrong? At any cost let me have her, that is if she will take me for better or worse."

Edward Colston looked with his old keen glance at the young man, and said:

"You know she is the inheritor of the

greater portion of my wealth. The time must be near for me to depart hence. Five worthy men are appointed trustees; and then the man who is her husband takes her name."

Hyacinth Aldworth interrupted him.

"You do not surely misjudge me, sir. You do not know of what stuff I am made."

A spasm of wounded pride passed over Hyacinth's fine face, and Edward Colston held out his hand to him.

"Nay, do not take it amiss," he said; "but I say to you now, my will is made, and cannot be altered. All earthly settlements are over for me. Since I lost my sister, the last tie to the old generation is broken—broken here— to be united in a better life. Thus your name will not be written in the will; but as I said, Sarah will inherit the largest portion of that which God has suffered me to acquire."

"You have already done so much for me, sir," Hyacinth Aldworth said. "The time I passed in the Law Courts here was not in vain. I returned to Pennsylvania to provide every comfort for my mother, and I am accounted there as one whose opinion on all legal questions it is well to seek. Thus, sir, I need nothing at your hands, or any man's;

and I only seek your leave to tell Sarah of my love."

"You can never transplant so tender a plant to that distant country. If she lives, you must promise me to abide here."

"I promise; for I have none there to desire me greatly, since my mother was laid to rest."

"Well, then, we understand each other; be not too hasty or eager with the child. She is a flower that can ill bear a rough breath."

"You may trust me," was the reply, "and I hope I am right when I believe the flower will raise its head to the sun when she is sheltered from all rude blasts, by my protecting love."

There was need of but few words or pleading entreaty. The child's love was ready for Hyacinth, and, as is often the case, the entire happiness and trust Sarah felt seemed to woo her back to life.

Still she never talked of the future, and one day when they were alone together, she drew her Bible and Prayer Book from under the cushions of her couch, and said:

"Uncle Edward gave me these, so I have written your name in them, Hyacinth."

"That is well," he said; "but why not wait till one name serves for us both?"

"Why? because it is ever better to live in the present, nor to look so far. The present is so happy, and the future may not come. So remember that I wrote your name under mine in these precious books as a Christmas gift, if you will." And then she smiled on him and said, "Do not look so grave. Let us be happy with the love God has given us. See, I will get Pepita to bring my wrap, and I will take a turn with you by the river. It is always sunny there."

Pepita brought her wrap, and well muffled in fur, Sarah stepped forth, leaning on Hyacinth's arm. It was a soft December day, mild and balmy; it was hard to believe that it was mid-winter.

"It is beautiful here," Sarah said, as they turned into the dry gravel path; "and how fair the river looks! I have walked here many a time, Hyacinth, thinking of you; and I used to drop a leaf upon the silvery water, and tell it to go out upon the swift-running tide to the ocean, and bear my love with it."

"Sweetheart!" Hyacinth said, "please God we part no more."

"And if we do—if I have to cross the river that the pilgrims crossed in the beautiful story I love to read, then I shall send messages from the great ocean of love back to you, till you come to me."

"Nay, do not talk in this sad strain, Say; you are so much stronger and better. When I first came home you could not take a step beyond the path by the house. You are getting quite well."

And yet as he said it, he wished she did not lean quite so heavily upon his arm, and he wished that she did not breathe quite so quickly as she walked.

"But she will be well in the spring," he said to himself, "and we shall be married in April."

Christmas came and went, and several relatives were invited to Mortlake, to keep the great Christian festival.

There was an immense quantity of roasting and boiling going on in the spacious kitchens.

"Let the poor folk have a double feast this year, to show my gratitude for a double blessing. My child Sarah is better, and Hyacinth is as a son to me. Yes, let it be a double feast, for methinks it will be my last on earth. And with so many vacant places I feel the time must be coming near when mine also shall know me no more." So said Edward Colston to his faithful Pepita, who was going over the preparations with her master according to time-honoured custom. "I feel like one left without a counsellor now Master Jones is gone. Forty years have we been friends, and forty years he has fed me with the bread of life. His loss and sister Ann's leave behind a sore blank."

"Yes, indeed," said Pepita; "I know, my dear master, all you feel, but you have yet many left to revere and honour you. There's but few folks who have so many voices at Christmastide to call them blessed as you have."

"Aye, good Pepita, that may be so; but true peace comes only from the Fountain of Peace, even from the cross of Christ. I feel, if I lose all else, I must hold to that with all my failing strength."

Sarah seemed wonderfully well on Christmas Day. She came down ready dressed for church with a bright smile, and her silvery voice as she wished everyone a "Merry Christmas" was like the sweetest music.

She was carried in a sedan chair to the church, Hyacinth walking by her side. The chair was brought into the hall, and thus she was protected from cold.

The close old-fashioned chariot conveyed

Edward Colston and Sophia Edwards, and one of the daughters of the Rector of St. Werburgh, Bristol, who had come to partake of the hospitalities of Mortlake at this season.

Mrs. Elizabeth Beavis and a clergyman, Mr. James, joined the party at the mid-day dinner. The hospitable board literally groaned under the weight of silver upon it, and the massive sideboard was also glittering with plate. In the large kitchen, huge quantities of beef and pudding had been dispensed to the poor, and a few of these, whom Mistress Pepita had singled out as most worthy, were invited to dine with the lower members of Edward Colston's household.

Sarah sat at the head of the table next her uncle, and it was beautiful to notice her attention to him, for his sight was failing, and gently and unobtrusively a little white hand would guide the aged one to the silver cup or the plate, or tell him in a low voice what viands were on the table. Opposite sat Hyacinth. He could scarcely take his eyes off his 'princess,' as he called her, and Mrs. Beavis, who belonged to the family of Job's comforters, remarked to Hyacinth:

"You think Sarah looks better. Yes; but

see, she does but play with her knife and fork, and that colour in her face is a deal too bright: it tells a sad tale."

Hyacinth disliked Mrs. Beavis from that moment, and to Sarah's surprise expressed his opinion after dinner that "she was a meddling old idiot;" and that he thought she was a great deal too often in the house, for her room was better than her company.

"Uncle Edward likes her," Sarah said; "she is very kind to him, and since I have had this cough she has taken my place in reading to him. She is a very good woman, Hyacinth."

"A pity she isn't a more agreeable one then," was the reply. "Nay, sweet one, do not look so grieved. I will kiss her under the mistletoe fifty times if it will please you."

Early in February Hyacinth left Mortlake for Bristol, and was charged by Edward Colston with several business commissions there. It was hard to Hyacinth to leave Sarah; but she seemed well and bright, and even spoke of the future more definitely, saying:

"When I am thy wife I shall ride to Bristol with thee, Hyacinth. We will have a soft-cushioned pillion, and an old nag, sure footed and steady, like the one Mistress Carr rides; and if we meet highwaymen, why, I know well what a valiant protector I shall have."

She spoke gaily, and followed him into the hall, the musk-coloured mantle, with its squirrel lining, wrapt round her, and on her head she wore a peaked velvet hood edged with gold, which suited her well.

"God keep thee!" Hyacinth said, as he turned again and again, to clasp her in his arms.

"God keep thee, dear one! and have a care of the wind, for it is cold and biting."

"Yes," exclaimed Pepita, "and Say standing here with the door open! Run back, child, to the drawing-room, and watch thy 'lover ride away.'"

With one more kiss, Sarah obeyed, skipping up the few wide stairs, and calling, "Good-bye. See, I can run now as of old."

She found her uncle in his chair drawn by James close to the window, which commanded a view of the drive, where, well mounted, with well-filled saddle bags, and rapier, and loaded musket, Hyacinth was riding slowly towards the old stone gate, followed by a servant, mounted on a trusty cob, which had often taken the journey to Bristol.

Hyacinth looked back, and took off his plumed hat with all his old grace. The sweet face watching from the window gazed wistfully after his retreating figure, and then putting her arms round her uncle's neck, Sarah said, "It is a long Good-bye."

"He is gone only for a short space, dear child. So trustworthy a messenger, with so clear a head, will speedily transact my business. When he returns we will set about other preparations."

"Yes," she said, "when he returns;" and then she kissed her uncle's forehead, and said, "All things are well to those who love God."

"Yes, dear child, and, blessed be His name, I am at peace in that Faith, peace that the world cannot give, little Sarah."

A fortnight later, and a horseman rode wildly up the drive, pulling up his horse on its haunches, within a few yards of the house.

"Lest the ring of the hoofs should startle her," he said, as he leaped off, and left his man servant to catch the bridle, of which he took no heed.

The old house was very quiet as Hyacinth

opened the door of the Hall and went softly in. No one met him, and he ascended the few shallow stairs to the corridor, on which the bedrooms opened.

His steps were heard by Pepita, who came out of a room to the right, with a face which bore the traces of many tears.

"Am I too late?" Hyacinth asked.

"She is gone, dear master, she is gone!"

Hyacinth clasped his hands together, as if to control the great agony of his heart.

"Why did you not warn me earlier?"

"We sent post-haste as soon as it happened; we could do no more," said poor Pepita, struck with fear by Hyacinth's face.

"What happened? you speak in riddles."

He leaned heavily against the balustrade as if to support himself.

"The dear child had a bleeding from her mouth on Sunday. She had felt so well, she had walked from church, and dismissed the chair. The day was mild and sunny."

"And you let her do this? I can never forgive you."

Then Hyacinth drew himself erect, for slow and feeble steps were heard approaching, and Edward Colston came towards him.

"Dear boy," he said, laying his hand within Hyacinth's arm, "mourn not too bitterly for her; she is at rest."

"For her? Ah! no; but oh! my life, my life without her, you cannot know."

Edward Colston smiled sadly.

"I have lived fourscore and five years, and I *do* know; come and look at her as she lies asleep."

So the old man, who was standing on the brink of the grave, and the young man in the prime of his manhood, went together to the room where all that was mortal lay of Sarah Colston.

"It is too hard, too hard to lose her," Hyacinth exclaimed, throwing himself on his knees by the side of the maiden, who, like one in that upper chamber of Judea, long ago, looked as if the Master's words again might be verified: 'She is not dead, but sleepeth.'

To the old man, who had life lying far behind him, and death so near, the keen edge of sorrow like Hyacinth's might perhaps be blunted. But as he gazed on the fair young face, where a smile seemed yet to linger, another vision rose before him out of the vanished years, a dark vaulted chamber in the old house in St. Mary le Port Street, Bristol. And another face turned up to his, seemed to bear upon it the same assurance of death and blessed hope of immortality.

"Take comfort," Edward Colston said, laying his hand on Hyacinth's bowed head. "Take comfort, and lay to your heart those words of vital power—'I believe in the life everlasting.'"

They laid the child to rest in the church of All Saints, Bristol, where her kindred were buried, and soon after Hyacinth Aldworth set out again for the New World, to settle his affairs in Pennsylvania, intending to return to Mortlake to minister to his friend and benefactor, who was now bound to him by the strongest ties. But this intention was never carried out. Rest came to the weary long before it was possible for Hyacinth to return. The news of Edward Colston's death reached him by the hand of his true and faithful friend Mr. James, and Hyacinth Aldworth never set foot on English soil again.

Mr. James, who knew how tenderly Hyacinth had loved Sarah, and how steadfast had been his allegiance to Edward Colston, undertook, at Hyacinth's request, to write a short account of the last days of one, who had been a true friend to both.

It may not be inappropriate to reproduce this letter, which is written with evident feeling, and is free from the fulsome adulation, which too often characterised similar effusions of that kind, when the death of a man who had made any mark in his day and generation, seemed to be the signal for extravagant eulogy, under which facts were often buried as pearls, beneath drifts of sand, or gold in heaps of dross.

The letter, which was evidently written at intervals, was as follows:

" Endorsed.

" From Pascal James, Clerk in Holy Orders, a resident in Mortlake, Surrey, to Hyacinth Aldworth, of High Woods, Pennsylvania,

"January, 20, 1722.

"Honoured sir,

" The short letter, written by me on the day following the death of our dear and trusty friend, Mr. Edward Colston, will have apprised you of the call to rest which none who loved him could desire to be long delayed.

" I have thought often of those words in the Book of Job, 'As the servant desireth the shadow.' For our friend, though patient and uncomplaining, did certainly desire the rest which remaineth, and the call which, after long labour in the harvest field of his Lord and Master, he answered humbly yet gladly, *bearing his sheaves with him.*

"It seemed to me and to all who were with him daily, that after the death of that dearly loved one, for whom you also, dear sir, mourned sorely, that Mr. Colston's steady decline set in. I scarcely think he set foot out of doors more than twice, or at most, three times during the summer. He was last in the church at Mortlake on the Christmas Day you know of.

"But do not think that he was, therefore, shut out from the consolation of the Church he loved, for he remarked, 'Business is irksome, and even thought wearies; but prayer is ever welcome.' The Collects of the Church he would speak of as containing 'the very marrow of Godliness.'

"Of late but few neighbours or friends were admitted to his room. Mistress Elizabeth Beavis ministered to him with a willing heart, and his housekeeper, good Pepita, was not behindhand in her labour of love. As for myself, dear sir, I accounted it an honour to be continually near our friend, and he was pleased to say that he felt satisfaction in my presence. While life lasts, I shall ever have before me that eleventh day of October, when the last hours of this valued life on earth were told out. For I guard myself, honoured sir, with those words *life on earth*. Can we doubt that his faith, expressed often times in the words of the Creed, was vain? No, he has but exchanged the mortal for the immortal life.

"It would seem to the bystanders that he saw in that still chamber of death, angel faces which we saw not. For there passed over his countenance now and again, as if he recognised some friend, a smile of greeting. We heard familiar names—mother, Nan, dear Ned, evidently the much-loved nephew, the father of his little Sarah.

"No names were those of the living; therefore you may not take it amiss that your own, dear sir, was not among them. He always coupled Sarah, 'little Say,' with another—that other strange to me and Mrs. Beavis. But this last name, repeated with an eager upturned gaze, was that of Damaris, and something like a murmur, 'Damaris, I am coming.'

"Then at intervals he would say, 'Not unto us, O Lord, not unto us, but unto Thy name be the praise, for Thy loving mercy and truth's sake.' So with a prayer half articulate on his lips he passed away, entering into the life everlasting.

"As you may be aware, he left full instructions for his funeral, and as far as possible they were obeyed.

"At his request also, leave was sought from his Grace the Archbishop of Canterbury to remove the body of Mistress Ann Colston from the vault at Mortlake, to rest with those of her kindred in All Saints' Church at Bristol.

"For myself, I could have wished that there had been less of the pomp of a funeral; but though my heart did not beat in unison with the show of plumes and velvet, of twelve pages, in black, with caps and truncheons, and so forth, yet at Bristol the solemnity of the occasion thrilled through my very heart, as those who had shared his bounty met all that was mortal of their benefactor.

"But to return to some details which at the distance of half the world, may not come amiss to you, dear sir, the long train set forth in the early morning from Mortlake, and I was a humble unit therein. Time would fail me to tell of the crowds upon the road.

"At Brentford where all halted, a funeral chamber was prepared, hung with black, and wax candles in heavy sconces burning. A like chamber was prepared also in other places, for, dear sir, we were a full week upon the road.

"Methinks there never was a drearier day than that November day, when at last we drew near the old city of Bristol. To add to the doleful character of the scene, the rain fell in one ceaseless downpour. The plumes were weighted with moisture, the attendants robed in black that walked beside the hearse were a sorry spectacle, so drenched were their garments, and the silver edged escutcheons, and the banners were marred indeed.

"Not till midnight did the sound of the bells of the Cathedral and city churches, borne upon the air, tell that Bristol was reached.

"And now at Lawford's gate, by the light of the torches, which cast on all around a lurid glare, as wreaths of mist surrounded them, caused by the rain, through which it was hard to keep them burning bright—I beheld a throng, which told a story of the life and service of the departed, which must needs leave its mark upon all who saw it.

"A solemn chant rose from the lips of the

boys who had been instructed in the words of the Ninetieth Psalm, and as the procession halted at the said Lawford's gate, the sound of those blessed words fell upon the ear with wondrous power.

"' Lord, Thou hast been our refuge from one generation to the other,' and on in measured cadence from the first word to the last. 'Show Thy servants Thy work, and their children Thy glory: and the glorious majesty of the Lord our God be upon us: prosper Thou the work of our hands upon us, O prosper Thou our handy-work.'

"These young ones in the springtime of their days, chanting the solemn words, touched many to the quick. There were besides, the hundred boys from the Hospital on St Augustine's Back, the six boys maintained at Queen Elizabeth's Hospital, in the College Green, and the forty boys from the Temple Parish, under the care of Mr. Carey, who succeeded that excellent man, Mr. Bedford, who so unhappily broke with our friend at the election in 1710, but who had full forgiveness of the wrong, as it seemed at the time, a wrong never to be forgotten.

"But, dear sir, if it was a moving spectacle

as the young filed past, who shall describe the effect produced as the twenty-four aged men and women from St. Michael's Hill, and the six poor sailors, came feebly onward in their proper order, protected by the stout gowns and coats which—precise in the smallest details as in the largest—Mr. Edward Colston had ordered to be proved for the occasion?

"Many thousands of people lined the streets as the procession passed, and the houses and church towers of St. Werburgh and St. Stephen were illuminated by the same lurid glow from innumerable torches.

"At last All Saints was reached, and, as he had willed, the burial service of the Church was read, in a solemn and feeling manner, by the reverend and esteemed rector, Doctor James Harcourt. So in the vault, where one you know of, in her youth and loveliness, was hidden from sight, not nine months ago, the massive coffin was placed side by side with that of Mrs. Ann Colston, and it may be said with no ordinary force, 'their bodies rest in peace, but their souls live for ever.'

"It was a strange burial, and such as the city of Bristol will scarce ever see again.

"For me, I found my way back to Mortlake

COLSTON'S MONUMENT.

with a sad heart. The desolation of the house is pain to me As you well know, dear sir, she who was to have been mistress of all things there, has entered upon an immortal heritage, verily, incorruptible and undefiled, which fadeth not away.

"Mr. Francis Colston has been here settling for the division of the rich plate, India chests, cabinets, china, and so forth. As to the fair orange trees and evergreens, in which our departed friend took such pride, I know not what will befall them.

"Indeed I can tell you but little more.

"That house which once I entered secure of welcome, is now, as it were, closed to me. Mrs. Elizabeth Beavis is at one with me in the feeling of strangeness where once all was familiar and home-like. She is remembered in the will, but let that pass.

"One incident speaketh volumes. As I passed the great gate to-day, seated in one of the stone niches, I saw a poor woman, her head bowed on her hands, weeping bitterly. On questioning her as to her grief, she said,

"'Alas! good sir, I have come from a distant part to ask the help of one, who never turned his face from any poor man. I have a brave son languishing in gaol for debt, which never can he pay. They told me that Mr. Colston would set him free as a bird, as he had before done many sad debtors, who pined in durance from no crime or fault. Alas! good sir,' said the poor creature, 'I heard at the house that Master Colston is dead and in his grave. They shut the door on me, and I am foot-sore and famished.'

"I led the poor creature to my own humble home, and gave her what help lay in my power; but, alas, indeed, that he who never, as she said, turned his face from any poor man, should be beyond the cry of the poor destitute! May God raise up others in his place, who will dispense their wealth for the benefit of the poor, and so lay up for themselves treasures in heaven. May Bristol merchants take this to heart. Methinks there is great need.

"And now, dear and honoured sir, it only remains for me to assure you of my respectful esteem, and that I am,

"Your obedient servant and friend,

"PASCAL JAMES."

UNIVERSITY OF CALIFORNIA LIBRARY
Los Angeles
This book is DUE on the last date stamped below.

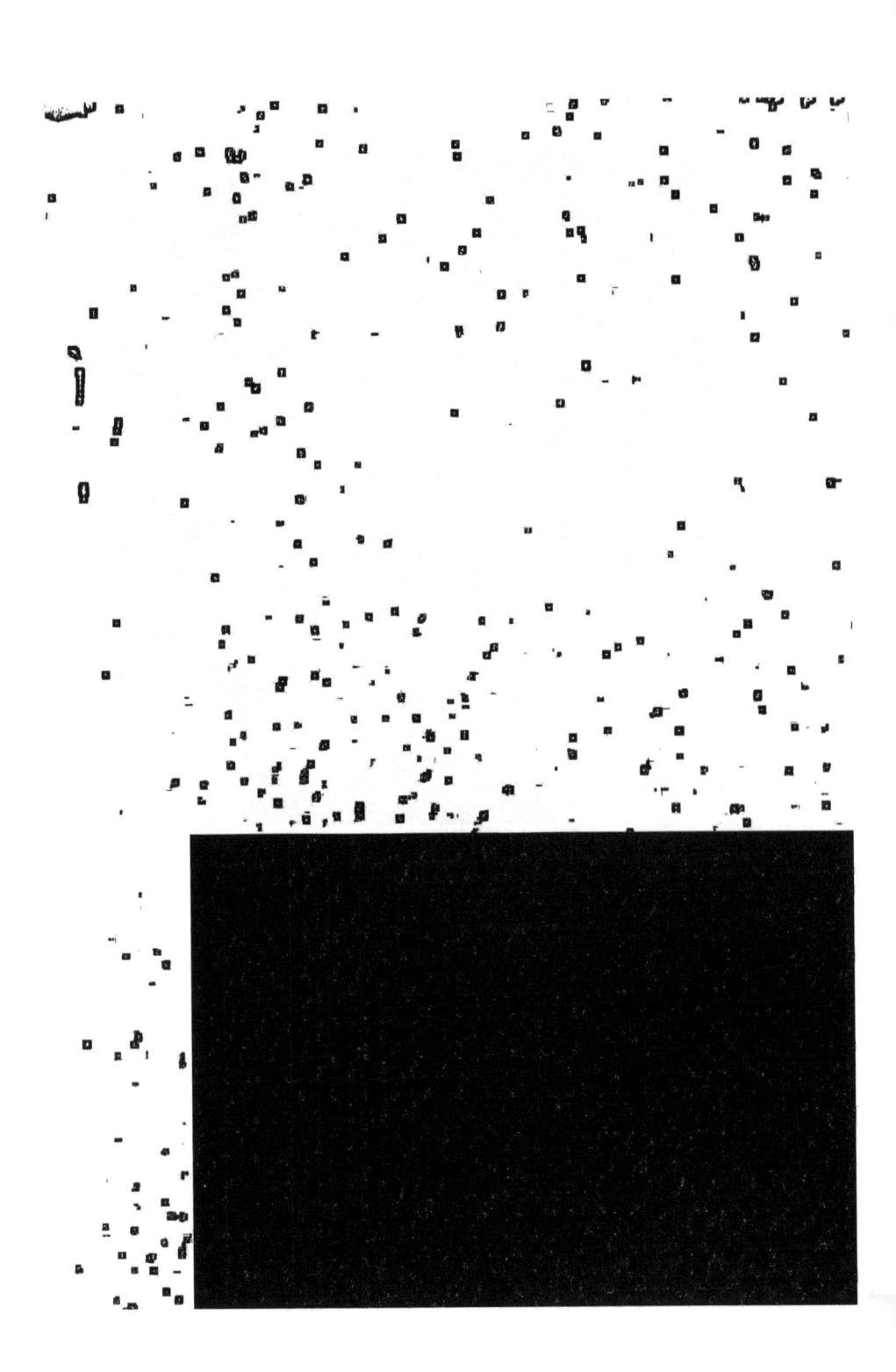